Scenarios II

Also by Werner Herzog
Published by the University of Minnesota Press

Of Walking in Ice

*Scenarios: Aguirre, the Wrath of God |
Every Man for Himself and God Against All |
Land of Silence and Darkness | Fitzcarraldo*

Scenarios II

Signs of Life
Even Dwarfs Started Small
Fata Morgana
Heart of Glass

Werner Herzog

Translated by
Krishna Winston and Werner Herzog

University of Minnesota Press
Minneapolis | London

Published by the University of Minnesota Press
111 Third Avenue South, Suite 290
Minneapolis, MN 55401–2520
http://www.upress.umn.edu

Printed in the United States of America on acid-free paper

The University of Minnesota is an equal-opportunity educator and employer.

24 23 22 21 20 19 18   10 9 8 7 6 5 4 3 2 1

Library of Congress Cataloging-in-Publication Data
Herzog, Werner, author. | Winston, Krishna, and Werner Herzog, translators.
Scenarios II : Signs of Life, Even Dwarfs Started Small, Fata Morgana, Heart of Glass / Werner Herzog ; translated by Krishna Winston and Werner Herzog.
First University of Minnesota Press edition. | Minneapolis : University of Minnesota Press, 2018. |
Identifiers: LCCN 2018001925 (print) | ISBN 978-1-5179-0441-8 (pb)
Classification: LCC PN1998.3.H477 A25 2018 (print) | DDC 791.43/75–dc23
LC record available at https://lccn.loc.gov/2018001925

Contents

The screenplay for *Signs of Life* was written in 1964 and originally bore the title *Signs of Fire*. The film was not shot until 1967, on the Greek islands of Kos and Crete, right after the military takeover. Just as the title was altered, many changes occurred while the film was being shot and edited, including some that took the work in a very different direction. To give only one example, the key image of the ten thousand windmills does not appear in the original screenplay because at the time they played no part in my conception of the film. In preparing the text for publication, I decided not to add the dialogue list from the actual film for purposes of comparison; this version was not intended to represent a working script.

The idea for *Even Dwarfs Started Small* came to me in 1966, but the screenplay was not written until the end of 1967. Then in 1968 and 1969, I first shot the major portions of *Fata Morgana* in East Africa and the Sahara, and at the end of 1969 I filmed the dwarf movie on the Canary Island of Lanzarote. But that film was edited and completed first, followed by *Fata Morgana*. I never wrote an actual screenplay for that film; it was to meant to be a science fiction story. That explains why the version in this volume consists only of the complete dialogue list. The Creation section was taken, with slight modifications, from the *Popol Vuh*, a sixteenth-century text from Guatemala. My friend Manfred Eigendorf collaborated with me on the other two sections.

W. H.
Munich, 8 March 1977

Postscriptum

I always felt it odd that each shot is numbered in the screenplay of *Signs of Life*, but at the time I wrote it I had never seen a screenplay. Someone told me that a proper scenario had to include numbers, otherwise it would not be professional. There is a certain innocence in my having followed this advice, and I thought the scenario should stay as it has always been.

As to the central images of the ten thousand windmills: they were dormant in me since I saw them as a fifteen-year-old adolescent traveling on foot the length of the Greek island of Crete. I remember clearly that I omitted the windmills in the written text because I thought every viewer of the film would immediately know that I had wildly constructed the geography—these images could not have been shot on the small island of Kos, so their origin hence was misrepresented. Obviously, virtually no one among all audiences I have had for the film would have known or cared about it.

Regarding *Even Dwarfs Started Small*, the text does not have the full ashen despair of the film itself, as it became more radical during shooting. At that time, I was totally convinced I would not live to be twenty-five, but after this hurdle was taken and I turned twenty-six, I asked myself: if I had such an unexpected extension of life, should I not be at least as bold as Goya when he was old, sensing the grip of the Reaper? His darkest, his greatest, most nightmarish visions were painted in the series of Black Paintings. Goya gave me the courage to turn my film into a vortex of laughter and despair.

As to *Heart of Glass,* I always sensed there was a somnambulistic quality to the behavior of the villagers in the story. They walk into a prophesied, foreseen disaster like sleepwalkers. I thought they should act in real trance. In fact, I cast the film carefully with actors who would be willing to follow me in a completely new terrain—to act under hypnosis. First tests confirmed that people deep in the state of hypnosis could open their eyes without "waking up" and that they could communicate with each other in dialogue. I had to dismiss a professional New Age creep of a hypnotist who maintained there was a "cosmic aura" that he, by dint of his special powers, could attract and radiate onto "subjects," thus hypnotizing them. After two sessions, I had to do it alone, and during shooting I had to be the hypnotist. Further, since we do not know much about perception and vision, out of curiosity I conducted tests with audiences in a movie theater whom I put under hypnosis. They saw films and had very strange experiences. As there are certain psychological risks in this, I did not follow up with my experiments.

For *Fata Morgana,* the texts emerged only during the phase of editing—in a way, they imposed themselves onto the footage of the film. While I was filming mirages in the Sahara Desert, I had a vague feeling that what I saw felt like the Creation of the World abandoned by its Creator. And it was almost natural that the images also had a forlorn Paradise and an anguished Golden Age embedded in them—waiting to be named, to be lifted, to be redeemed.

Today, I still marvel at the film. I knew I was not making a documentary (some critics who have lost all hope in cinema are trying to label it as such). I remember that on the first day of editing, my editor, Beate Mainka-Jellinghaus, to whom I owe a lot, said that with this kind of material we have to pretend to invent cinema. I continue to try to do this today.

Los Angeles, 1 December 2017

Signs of Life

——— ——— ———

Landscape on Crete

1. Tracking shot, facing backward from a truck toiling along a dusty road in the mountains of Crete. Ceaseless, piercing chirping of cicadas. The land is typical karst and scorched by the sun. Rocks, dust, and now and then olive trees, stone walls marking the boundaries of fields, uninviting, struggling farmsteads. A lone rider mounted sideways on a donkey that is also carrying heavy panniers. The rider's legs bob in rhythm with the donkey's gait, slapping gently against the animal's sides. Parched fields.

2. Sideways traveling shot: olive trees in the afternoon heat.

3. Looking backward: passing a flock of sheep huddled by the roadside. The shepherd lolling nearby. The first few houses of a small village. The cicadas' chirping falls silent.

Village

4. Long shot from in front. A confiscated Greek army truck drives into the village and stops by one of the first houses.

5. Medium long shot. The driver and passenger, two youngish German soldiers, jump down from the cab and turn their attention to the truck's canvas-covered bed.

6. A third soldier, up on the bed, parts the canvas flaps. The other two soldiers move in close.

FIRST SOLDIER: What's wrong? Why did you want us to stop?

THIRD SOLDIER: It's so hot under the canvas. We have to get him out. He can't breathe in here.

7. The house by which the truck has stopped. It's whitewashed, and joined to it is a wall with a rather low opening through which one can see into the small courtyard, half-covered by a pergola. An older woman in dark clothing appears in the opening, behind her a girl of about twenty. The woman emerges, looking half-curious, half-fearful.

THE WOMAN (in Greek): Are you looking for us?

The soldier to whom she addressed the question doesn't understand and shrugs.

8. Medium close-up. The truck from behind. Two stretchers are on the bed, each with a man on it. Only the feet can be seen: on the stretcher to the left the feet are in hobnailed Wehrmacht boots. The man on the right-hand stretcher is dead, covered by a blanket. The soldier standing on the bed hands down his rifle, then lifts the head end of the stretcher slightly and slides it toward the back edge of the bed.

9. Camera from the side. The two soldiers on the ground reach for the foot of the stretcher. In the background the woman.

SECOND SOLDIER: Don't let him fall off. He's heavier than he looks.

They lower the stretcher and set it on the ground.

10. Medium close-up. The stretcher seen from above, at an angle. On it lies Stroszek, seriously wounded, with a wide bandage around his head. He's barely thirty, gaunt, with sharp features. He lies there quietly, his eyes open.

11. Long shot. The third soldier jumps down from the bed and turns to the woman. He speaks to her in Greek.

THIRD SOLDIER (in Greek): Good day. We have a sick man here. Can we take him inside?

WOMAN (in Greek): Come in. I'll get you some water.

Meanwhile the girl—it's Nora—has already come out with a ceramic pitcher of water. As she approaches the group she tips the pitcher to moisten a cloth with which she then dabs Stroszek's face.

FIRST SOLDIER: Good girl!

She seems to understand him.

12. Close-up from above at an angle. Stroszek turns his head a bit toward Nora and his mouth opens, but he can't speak. Nora is quite small. She has very dark eyes. Her eyebrows almost meet above the root of her nose.

Small Courtyard

13. Inside the courtyard. The stretcher is carried in and put down in the shade of the pergola. The paving stones have been sprinkled with water against the heat. All around are large tin containers holding a profusion of flowers and plants. A whitewashed exterior staircase leads up to the house. The kitchen is at ground level, its door open.

14. Medium close-up. The door to the kitchen, into which the woman has disappeared. She brings out two chairs.

15. In one corner are a bench and a small table. The woman sets the chairs down by the table.

WOMAN (in Greek): Have a seat, gentlemen!

THIRD SOLDIER (in Greek): Thank you so much!

16. Medium close-up. Nora carefully lifts Stroszek's head, pulls out the folded Wehrmacht coat that has been serving as a pillow, and places a real pillow under his head.

17. Long shot. The courtyard from the entrance. The soldiers are sitting at the small table, having shed their jackets. From the kitchen the woman brings wine, bread, and glasses.

THIRD SOLDIER (in Greek): Oh, thank you, that wasn't necessary.

WOMAN (in Greek): Go ahead and drink; it's so hot out. It'll do you good.

She fills the glasses and pushes one toward each soldier. Nora comes to the table.

18. Close-up. Nora picks up the bottle, moistens her cloth with wine, and returns to Stroszek. The camera follows her. She dabs his parched lips. He continues to lie there apathetically.

19. Medium close-up. The woman watches the soldiers for a while, then pulls herself together.

WOMAN (in Greek): You have another man on the truck. He's dead, and I will light a candle for him. The Blessed Mother of God will care for him.

20. Close-up: Stroszek's face. His eyes are half-open.

21. Loud chirping of cicadas. Parts of shots 1–3, but in reverse order, with the result that the flock of sheep comes toward the camera, for instance. Karst landscape with fields.

Ano Archanes, Village Square

22. Long shot. A larger Cretan village. Square with several trees that have spreading canopies. Under them *kafenion* chairs. Bums dozing, stretched across two chairs. Oppressive heat. A couple of men are playing a board game; no women. A bus in the middle of

the square. No sounds but the ceaseless chirping of cicadas until shot 26.

23. Long shot. Looking from the *kafenion* toward the bus, with about twelve passengers waiting to get on. Wicker hampers covered with cloths are being tied on to the roof. A couple of sheep are hoisted into the back. From far in the background a German military patrol (two men) approaches. No one pays much attention to them.

24. Medium long shot. Three donkeys are standing sleepily in the shade by the *kafenion*, their saddles removed, flicking their ears. Suddenly they all flinch (reacting to shots fired, not on the soundtrack). A quick pan across the entire square to where the two soldiers have collapsed. The people waiting by the bus flee, seeking shelter in the houses.

25. The camera zooms in on the two soldiers. One is laying on his back, dead, his arms outstretched. His helmet has rolled away to the rear, and his whole chest is drenched in blood. Next to him lies Stroszek, seriously wounded, propping himself on one arm and trying to raise his head. But he collapses completely from the effort.

26. Medium long shot. The abandoned bus. The two sheep jump out of the rear door, which was left open, and stand there confused.

27. From the middle of the square. The *kafenion* is empty, one chair knocked over.

28. Long shot. From the *kafenion*. A Jeep drives into the empty square at high speed. The two soldiers are hastily loaded into the Jeep and driven away. The square is deserted.

29. The first few villagers venture out of the houses.

30. Some of them approach the spot where pools of blood can be seen.

31. Long shot. A Jeep races into the square, followed by a truck. Both stop. Most of the people flee again. Soldiers jump out of the vehicles and arrest the first four men they can get hold of. The men scramble onto the truck without resisting. The vehicles drive off.

Ano Archanes, the Schoolyard

32. Long shot. The schoolyard, enclosed on two sides by a white-washed stone wall. The last few children go into the school building as recess ends.

33. The open classroom windows. Inside the children are drawing the light-colored curtains against the harsh sun.

34. Long shot. From inside the school. The Jeep, followed closely by the truck, drives into the schoolyard and steers in an arc, stopping by the wall.

35. From the middle of the schoolyard. Three men with submachine guns come from the left, from the Jeep, and reach the back of the truck, where the unsuspecting four hostages are just jumping to the ground. Before they grasp what is happening, the three soldiers fire their weapons at close range. Only the first man, who has half-turned toward the soldiers, is struck in the front. Those behind him, struck from the side, fall to their knees, their heads jerking back. One of them still manages to stagger two steps, pressing his hands to his chest, before he too collapses.

36. Close-up. The wall of a medieval structure, its huge rectangular stones tightly joined. Among them is a much lighter stone, a piece of ancient marble with a well-preserved frieze. The cicadas fall silent.

Kos, the Harbor

37. Long shot. The small harbor of Kos. The harbor has a relatively narrow outlet, and only fishing boats and smaller freighters can get into the basin. On the left side is a breakwater with a small lighthouse at its tip, and on the right side of the harbor, on a spit of land, stands a squat, massive Venetian fortress. Boats are tied up across from the harbor entrance, on the side where the town is located, its edges extending almost to the fortress. A broad drive follows the curve of the harbor. On the inland side it is flanked by houses. Side streets branching off from it at right angles lead to the market square and to the center of town. But the town's life takes place entirely along the harbor drive, on the inland side of which are located the cafés, while on the harbor side the boats are loaded. Normal activity.

38. Medium shot. Stroszek and Meinhard, a sturdy middle-aged man with thinning hair, stroll past the *kafenion* chairs, both of their uniforms somewhat sloppy. Meinhard has a slight limp. The camera backs up as they move toward it.

MEINHARD: I still can't believe we've been posted here.

STROSZEK: Yes, this is the best place we could ask for. There's never been any real fighting here.

MEINHARD: I don't think there were any partisans here. And the people are fairly nice to us because they can tell we're losing the war.

They come to a *kafenion* and sit down at a table.

39. Camera from the side. The two soldiers sit next to each other with glasses of milky ouzo in front of them. They smoke as they watch the goings-on on the street. On one side of Stroszek's head there's still a patch where the hair hasn't grown back completely since he was wounded.

MEINHARD: But you haven't heard the best thing of all.

STROSZEK: What?

Meinhard takes a swig from his glass in order to savor the news.

40. Close-up. He puts the glass back on the ring he's left on the table.

41. Same shot as 39.

MEINHARD: The colonel wants to post us in the fortress to guard the depot. I heard the three men who've been there up to now are due to be relieved. So we're supposed to take over, along with another hero like us.

> Stroszek doesn't seem surprised.
> Suddenly he gives a strange laugh.

MEINHARD: There aren't a hundred soldiers on the entire front who have our kind of luck. I'm guessing it's mainly for your sake, so you can have your wife with you.

42. Frontal shot.

STROSZEK: Oh, I don't know about that.

He's somewhat disconcerted. He stubs out his cigarette on the table and gets up.

STROSZEK: Will you pay this time? I'm going to go sit on the breakwater for a while. . . . If you're right, I'll stand you a bottle of wine.

43. Long shot. Stroszek walks along the breakwater. The camera follows him. Fishing boats crowded together and small freighters, almost all of which have sails. Two boys sitting on the quay wall fishing have their backs to the camera. In the background one can make out the narrow harbor outlet.

44. Medium close-up. Stroszek goes up to the two boys, who are seven or eight. They glance up at him, then look away. They are suntanned, wearing short, overly wide pants, and are barefoot, with only washed-out undershirts on top. Their hair is shorn so close that their scalps are almost as brown as their shoulders.

Stroszek sits down beside them. They're fishing with ordinary string.

STROSZEK (in Greek): Caught anything today?

THE FIRST BOY (in Greek): Yes, three, and we haven't been here that long.

Stroszek sticks a cigarette in his mouth and offers the pack to the boys, who help themselves without a moment's hesitation. Then he hands them the box of matches. They all smoke in silence.

45. Close-up. A cork floats from the two fishing lines bobbing on the water. Hawsers of a freighter.

46. Same as 44. The three sit in silence. The second boy pulls his line out of the water, fastens a new bread cube onto the hook, and tosses it back in. The first boy feels a tug on his line.

47. The surface of the water. The cork has been dragged beneath the surface but is still visible. A light-colored fish about the length of a finger is thrashing on the hook. He pulls it out of the water.

48. Same as 44. The first boy pulls the fish toward him on the breakwater, removes the hook, grabs the fish by its tail, and casually strikes it two or three times on the rocky ground until it's dead.

49. Close-up. The fish is still jerking a little.

50. Same as 44. Stroszek tosses his cigarette butt into the water.

STROSZEK (in Greek): What kind of fish is that?

The first boy tells him its name.

51. The tied-up boats, with nets spread over them. Slow pan down to the water. The sides of boats, hawsers; the two cork floats bobbing on the surface. The cicadas begin to chirp.

Crete, a Small Town, Dusk

52. Long shot. The house where the transport for the wounded soldier made a stop. The truck starts up. In the door to the courtyard stands the older woman. Nora has come out of the house and stands motionless by the wall, her eyes following the truck.

53. Tight close-up. The narrow, silvery leaves of an olive tree. They stir slightly in the breeze.

54. Nora, in dark clothing, steps out of the courtyard and walks fast, heading in the direction in which the truck has disappeared. She's carrying a small bundle.

Crete, a Road

55. Nora trudges along the road. The camera follows her from one side, slightly ahead of her.

56. Long shot. From behind. Nora comes to a fork in the road. From one branch four peasant women approach, carrying bundles of chickens with their legs tied together. Nora goes up to them and asks them something.

57. Close-up. The peasant women are wearing dark kerchiefs on their heads, holding the ends of the kerchiefs on both sides in their mouths so only the upper parts of their faces remain uncovered. They point Nora in the right direction.

58. Close-up. The chickens. Their heads are drooping. Only a few of them still have the strength to raise their necks.

Crete, Iraklion, a Lively Street

59. Narrow, lively street. Fruit stands on either side. Teams of horses drawing wagons force their way through the crowds. Camera from above (from a house).

60. Same as 59. Closer. Nora enters the frame, trying to find her way.

Iraklion, Outside the Military Infirmary

61. A run-down flat-roofed schoolhouse. A sentry at the door initially prevents Nora from entering but then lets her in.

Iraklion, Inside the Military Infirmary

62. An almost bare room, which even with its sparse furnishings looks run-down. A blackboard on one wall reveals that this used to be a schoolroom. The paint is already peeling off the walls in a number of places. The camera pans across the room. Some distance away stand five beds, one of which is empty, while the others are occupied by wounded soldiers. Stroszek is on the far left. Nora is perched at the foot of his bed because there's no chair. She's brought grapes for him.

63. The camera pans from Nora to the wall, showing ink splatter, scribbles, and a handprint.

64. Stroszek is sitting half-upright in the bed, a wide pillow behind his back. He now has only a patch of gauze dressing on the side of his head, held in place by a narrow strip of adhesive. Nora is sitting close to him, feeding him his meal. She wipes a spoon clean on her dress.

65. From the side. Nora's eyes turn toward the door, and the camera pans in that direction. The older woman has entered, very agitated.

66. Medium close-up. Nora has stood up. The woman comes close to her and speaks insistently to her, although her gestures express uncertainty.

67. Medium close-up. From Stroszek's point of view. The woman is getting increasingly worked up. From the doorway the sentry comes over to her, trying to understand what is going on.

68. Close-up. The woman grabs Nora by the wrist and tries to drag her away.

69. Long shot. From Stroszek's point of view. Two of the other wounded sit up in bed and watch the scene. The one in the bed between them doesn't move; he's unconscious.

70. Long shot. From the side. The sentry takes hold of the woman and maneuvers her toward the door. He's still reluctant to throw her out completely. But when she struggles to get free, he takes charge and pushes her out. Nora tries to maintain her composure.

71. Medium long shot. From Stroszek's point of view. The woman forces her way in again and shakes her fists. The sentry finally gets her out of the room.

72. Close-up. Stroszek, who was sitting up in bed during the entire scene, now sinks back. His wound has started to bleed, soaking the gauze. Nora, who bends over him, pulls back in alarm and calls for help. The chirping of the cicadas grows softer.

Kos, the Harbor

73. Medium long shot. From one of the boats. Stroszek and the two boys are sitting on the dock. Music from a tavern. Stroszek has drawn up one leg and is supporting his arm on it. Next to him one of the boys is trying to bite through a knot at the end of his line. The other boy, somewhat younger, turns to Stroszek.

THE BOY (in Greek): Can I have another cigarette?

Stroszek lowers his raised leg in order to reach into his pants pocket more easily.

74. From the side. Stroszek offers him a cigarette.

STROSZEK (in Greek): Here, boys, help yourselves.

The camera pans from him to the street. Some distance away an older fisherman sits on the ground, surrounded by his spread-out nets.

75. The fisherman from close up. He's barefoot and has rolled his patched pants up to his calves. On top he's wearing an undershirt. A thick mat of chest hair extends up to the base of his throat. He has stretched a damaged place in the net between his two big toes and is nimbly repairing it with a spindle.

76. Nets with cork floats attached to them spread out on the ground.

Outside the Fortress

77. Long shot. The side with the entryway. Arching over an avenue lined with palm trees, a narrow bridge, partly shaded by trees, leads up to the gateway, which opens into the interior at about five meters above grade. The new members of the detail—Stroszek, Meinhard, and Becker, along with Stroszek's wife, Nora—are led in by one of the soldiers they are relieving.

78. On the bridge. The camera follows the group as it comes to the heavy iron-studded gate. Above the gate an old Venetian coat of arms. The soldier in the lead opens the gate.

Inside the Fortress

79. Interior. The group comes through the tunnel-like opening in the wall that forms the entryway. No one is carrying luggage. Becker, the third man in the new detail, is a fairly young soldier. His movements always seem rather awkward. The camera backs up in front of them. The soldier they are relieving fills them in on the routine.

SOLDIER: So let me give it to you straight. No need to knock yourselves out here. Guard duty— that's basically all there is to it. And it's only at night that it really matters.

80. Long shot. The fortress from the entryway. The width of the battlements along the top of the outer walls, which form a rectangle, reveals how solidly fortified the structure is. A broad ramp to one side of the entryway leads down into the inner courtyard with its sparse grass. The middle of the courtyard is occupied by several rather jumbled structures made of massive stone blocks and remarkably well preserved. In the right-hand corner across from the entryway stands a small house, built into the fortification wall. Next to it is the toolshed used by a restorer. The group is just coming down the ramp into the courtyard.

BECKER: How does that work, exactly?

SOLDIER: Someone has to be on patrol all night. We've tried various systems. The best way is to have one person on duty all night, and then he can take it easy during the day. The daytime patrols are covered by the unit responsible for the town. But even so, one . . . at least one member of the detail always has to be here.

81. From the front, at an angle. The group in the inner courtyard, with a chicken nearby.

SOLDIER: We still have two of our chickens here. They're the best layers. We roasted the others before we packed up.

STROSZEK: If we buy you a couple of bottles of wine, will you leave them here for us?

SOLDIER: All right, that's fine. But you should buy yourselves two or three more; otherwise, it's not worth the trouble.

MEINHARD: Where did you keep them penned?

SOLDIER: We let them run around. As long as the gate is closed, they can't get out. You just have to keep an eye out for where they build their nests. It's usually over there by the munitions depot. But sometimes they get ideas and go somewhere else entirely.

82. Medium long shot. Camera from the rear. The group of five has reached the structures inside the fortress that are in ruins. The soldier, followed by the others, opens a door in a massive stone building still in a very good state of preservation.

The Fortress, Inside the Munitions Depot

83. The soldier leads the new detail past shelves filled with crates containing munitions. The camera follows them.

SOLDIER: Most of this is for guns. It's not really worth keeping, since we don't use this caliber. It's the same with those grenades. The Greeks didn't have time to pick them up, and we use a different kind of launcher.

84. Close-up. Crates with lettering.

85. Close-up. The soldier goes over to the fuse box for the electrical system.

SOLDIER: Make sure no one smokes in here or fools around with the wiring. This stuff still packs a wallop. You could blow yourselves sky-high.

Courtyard of the Fortress

86. Long shot. From the middle of the courtyard. The group approaches the small building in the corner of the fortification. It's a squat structure, whitewashed, with large window shutters, all closed. Next to it is a flat-roofed shed, and nearby several pieces of ancient statues and chunks of marble are lying around.

Fortress, Inside the Cottage

87. Camera in the middle of the first room. The door from outside opens. The first person to enter the dim space is the soldier, who goes to the window and opens the shutters. The camera follows him.

88. Long shot. From the doorway. The cottage consists of two adjacent rooms, furnished relatively simply. Through the door into the back room one can see an open hallway that leads into a small kitchen.

SOLDIER: It's up to you to decide how you're going to use the rooms
.... This here's the kitchen. The only problem's the toilet; there
isn't one.

BECKER (laughs): Well, well!

SOLDIER: Over in the southwest corner we built a privy. I'll show
you later.

Courtyard of the Fortress

89. Close-up. Stroszek and the soldier are sitting by the battlements.

SOLDIER: The colonel will fill you in on general orders.

STROSZEK: How did it work for you?

SOLDIER: Nothing to worry about. You had to report daily, and that
was pretty much it. It's rare that you get any special orders. If all
goes well, you probably just have to make sure there's always one
of you in the fortress during the daytime.

90. Close-up. A marble pedestal with a weathered inscription in
Greek. On top the remnants of a statue—a toe and part of the
hem of a flowing garment.

The Fortress, Inside the Cottage

91. Stroszek and Nora in the back room, next to the kitchen. Nora
is busy hanging an icon over her bed.

STROSZEK: Do you like it here?

NORA: Yes, very happy—it's nicer than I would have thought. If we
stay a while, I'll have the baby into the world here.

STROSZEK: "I'll have the baby"—or "I'll bring it into the world." Not
all jumbled up.

NORA: What that means, "jumbled up"?

STROSZEK: Like this (he demonstrates with a gesture). Thrown
together, or something like that.

NORA: Maybe it is a son.

STROSZEK: You have to make an effort. By the time the war's over, we may have three.

92. Nora has hung the icon. She comes to Stroszek, who is sitting at the table, and leans up against him.

NORA: I not mad at the war. It brings you here.

93. The front room. It looks plainer than the back room because other than the table, chairs, and a wardrobe it has only small army cots. Meinhard is sitting on one of the cots polishing his boots. Becker is hunting for something.

BECKER: I can't find my fountain pen . . . . Have you seen it?

MEINHARD: No.

94. Medium shot. The camera follows Becker as he pokes around dispiritedly.

BECKER: It has to be here somewhere. I saw it just a minute ago.

MEINHARD: That's what you get for being a slob. Next thing you know, you'll lose track of your pants and will show up for inspection with a bare bottom.

BECKER: Spare me the jokes. Did you hide it from me?

MEINHARD: No. But you can have mine for now.

Meinhard gets up and graciously pulls his pen out of the pocket of his uniform jacket, which is on a hanger hooked over the wardrobe's door.

BECKER: Don't be a show-off. You're riding high now, but I'll show you yet.

95. Close-up. Becker starts writing. Suddenly he stops, looking agitated.

BECKER: Quick! Give me your hand.

Meinhard is taken aback and gives him his hand.

BECKER: Now pull!

The minute Meinhard pulls, Becker belches loudly. Meinhard is startled, but then he bursts out laughing. Becker begins to laugh, too. Both of them laugh hysterically.

96. The door opens and Stroszek pokes his head in.

STROSZEK: What's so funny?

97. Becker can hardly get a grip on himself. He mimes the pulling gesture.

BECKER: He . . . haha! He pulled.

Stroszek joins in the laughter.

98. Close-up. The camera pans to the wall and rests on a family photograph in which several people, rigidly posed by the photographer, stare solemnly straight ahead. The laughter dies down.

99. Medium long shot. In the back room all the members of the new detail are sitting at the table, waiting expectantly for the meal that Nora is bringing from the kitchen. Plates and slices of melon are already set out on the table.

NORA: Today not possible to cook properly. No salt and such.

MEINHARD: Oh, that doesn't matter. It'll taste good anyway.

NORA: We have wine, though. Retsina.

They eat and drink in silence for a while.

100. Close-up. Two cockroaches almost as large as June bugs skitter along the wall near the kitchen door.

101. Close-up. Meinhard, who is sitting facing the kitchen, catches sight of them. Stroszek follows his gaze. Meinhard gets up slowly and points at the floor.

MEINHARD: Oh, shit, this place is crawling with roaches.

STROSZEK: So what?

BECKER: They don't do any harm.

MEINHARD: They're the most disgusting creatures in existence. I've got to do something.

BECKER: But they can't even bite.

MEINHARD: No, but they drive me crazy, they're so disgusting. At night you hear them scraping and snapping the whole time; it's unbearable. Like this . . . (Meinhard holds up his left hand, pinching his thumb and index finger together and making a snapping noise with the nails) . . . and they keep it up all night long.

102. Close-up. A battered marble statue. Very stern, simple posture. The face is weathered. Blank eyes.

103. The front room. Becker is lying on his field cot half-asleep, barely covered. He gropes listlessly for a glass of water and sprinkles his chest and neck. To the right, near the head of his bed, Meinhard is kneeling on the floor.

104. Medium close-up. Meinhard from the side. Near the threshold between the two rooms he is busy setting up a complicated apparatus. He has fastened a bottle whose neck he has broken off to a gap between the baseboard and the wall, and inside the bottle he has placed a funnel-shaped ramp made of paper, creating a trap of sorts.

MEINHARD: This is the best way to catch roaches. They always keep close to the wall, like this . . . . See? They go in, but once they're inside they can't get out again . . . . Do you have any idea what they eat? I'll try sugar.

105. Same as 103. Becker doesn't answer because he's dozed off.

106. Same as 102. The ancient marble statue with blank eyes.

107. Medium long shot. The front room. It's morning, with the sky already bright. Meinhard is lying on his stomach on his cot, asleep. His arm dangles over one side. Becker is still dozing.

108. Stroszek, in a good mood and in full uniform, comes banging through the door from outside.

STROSZEK: Hey, you lazybones, time to get up!

Becker rolls out of bed but Meinhard continues lying there motionless. Stroszek goes over to his cot and shakes him. Meinhard makes an annoyed sound and doesn't budge.

STROSZEK: Come on, we have a lot to do today!

MEINHARD: To hell with both of you. Can't you see I'm dead?

109. Close-up. Becker gets his shaving kit and drapes a towel around his neck. Stroszek goes over to him.

STROSZEK: I'm telling you, I'm not even tired. Being out in the night on patrol is really, really nice. It's cool, and the stars give plenty of light. Over on the other side jellyfish came right up to the beach. They glow from inside. I saw at least ten of them.

110. From the side. Becker has caught sight of Meinhard's roach trap.

BECKER: Say, Meinhard . . . hey, Fritz, there are two of them in your trap.

MEINHARD: What!?

111. Meinhard leaps out of bed and carefully picks up the bottle. The two others crowd around him, full of curiosity.

112. Meinhard holds the bottle up in the air, as two large roaches scrabble agitatedly to climb up the side of the bottle but keep sliding back.

113. Medium long shot. Meinhard places the bottle on the table and turns toward the wardrobe.

MEINHARD: Wait, where's the DDT? . . . They need to get their dose.

Meinhard has found the canister and opens the lid.

114. Close-up. He carefully sprinkles DDT onto the two insects as if it were salt. They die quickly.

115. Tight close-up. The bottle with the dead roaches.

Courtyard of the Fortress

116. Long shot. At the front of the cottage Stroszek and Becker are busy painting the shutters with light-colored oil paint. To the left Meinhard is stretched out on a crude wooden bench in the shade of the toolshed. He's lying in a strangely contorted position, wearing only trousers and a shirt, his feet bare. Blazing heat. Flies buzzing, occasional cicada chirps. Stroszek stops painting.

STROSZEK: Don't we have any paint thinner or turpentine or such? The brushes keep getting clogged, and once they dry out they'll be useless.

BECKER: No. There's nothing here. But listen, wouldn't hot water work?

STROSZEK: I think the stuff's dried too much already.

BECKER: Then why don't we just use gasoline? I'm going into town in a little while, to go to the post office, and I'll bring some back.

117. Close-up. Rectangular stones in the fortress walls. Among the stones light-colored soles of two marble feet, the toes pointing up. They obviously belong to an ancient statue, used to fill a gap when the fortress was being constructed.

118. Medium long shot. Stroszek has already finished his shutter and has started to work on the one Becker was painting.

119. Meinhard on the bench. He has his eyes closed and with his toes is scrabbling and scratching at the wood of the bench.

120. Long shot. From the cottage. Becker comes across the courtyard hauling a canister. In the background a goat is staked. Chickens are also roaming around.

121. Stroszek pauses in his painting and turns toward Becker.

STROSZEK: What took you so long? I'm almost finished with yours.

BECKER: Those guys in procurement are such assholes. I tell them:
Listen, I need some gasoline, just a little, to clean our paint-
brushes. You'd think that would be a snap. But first they don't
want to open a full canister—regulations, you know—and then
they force me to take the whole thing, so heavy it almost did
me in.

STROSZEK: Oh, well, never mind. Let's get a move on. I can't take all
this hurry-up-and-wait.

122. Close-up. Becker, looking quite indignant, approaches Stroszek.

BECKER: What do you mean, get a move on? We haven't been here
even a week, and in two days tops there won't be anything left
for us to do.

MEINHARD'S VOICE: He's right. Two days from now, we'll have nothing to do but twiddle our thumbs.

Camera travels to Meinhard, who's joined the conversation.
Meinhard is sitting hunched over on the bench, still digging his
toes into the wood.

123. Medium long shot. One of the window shutters opens, and
Nora looks out.

NORA: Not to fight, please. No need for work to be so fast.

She leans out and kisses Stroszek soothingly on the forehead.

NORA: I'll bring you *rodakina*—how do you say?

STROSZEK: Peaches, one peach, two peaches.

124. Nora comes out of the door with a plate of peaches. The dress she is wearing plainly shows that she's pregnant. She hands out the peaches. All of them join Meinhard on the bench and bite into the fruit.

NORA: The goat give almost no milk! Must drink our coffee without milk.

BECKER: Aha!

MEINHARD: What do you mean, "Aha"?

BECKER: I warned you all from the beginning. First of all, goat milk is lousy because it has that billy-goat taste, and second, she isn't giving any now.

STROSZEK: You think we can sell her?

BECKER: Who would give us anything for her? They sold us a bill of goods, and no one's going to take her off our hands.

STROSZEK: Yes, it would've been better to spend the money for a few more chickens. But there's nothing we can do now.

NORA: Oh, with chickens is also hard. Hide all the eggs. Today here, tomorrow there.

125. Same as 90. A marble pedestal with a weathered inscription. On top remnants of a statue.

The Fortress, Inside the Cottage

126. The front room. Becker is sitting at the table writing while Meinhard is picking up his trap from the floor. First he clears a chair, which has a pile of clothes on it, then puts the bottle on the seat. Next he sprinkles in a pinch of DDT.

127. Close-up of Meinhard. He has the bottle in front of him on the chair. There's one roach in it.

MEINHARD: I need a different container. The neck of this bottle is so narrow that hardly any critters go in. Would you let me have your honey jar? That would be perfect.

128. Becker stops writing and fetches his honey jar from the wardrobe. The camera follows him.

BECKER: I don't mind. But put the rest of the honey in a cup . . . . I can't believe you're spending your time on this.

MEINHARD: What else is there to do? Feed the chickens and pull guard duty at night. That's all we're good for. And you, you sit there writing letters all the time. But you haven't received a single one. So why bother?

BECKER: That's my business. Wait and see, one of these days I'll get one.

129. Medium long shot. Meinhard pours the rest of the honey into a cup with a broken handle that he took from the windowsill. The honey flows sluggishly.

MEINHARD: Do you have this feeling, too? Something's not right here, but I'm not sure what.

BECKER: Yes, I feel the same. Actually, we're on top of the world, but somehow we're out of whack. There's the heat, and then it's not clear what we should be doing.

MEINHARD: The duty's so easy, but being on patrol all night isn't ideal. You never do catch up on sleep. You're not going to sleep past eleven or twelve, and then you stay up till late because that's when it finally cools down.

BECKER: I think this is no good for Stroszek either. He's so quick to fly off the handle. First he cracks the whip to get the work done, but then he's upset when there's nothing left to do. And recently—I wonder if you've noticed, too—he's been lacing into his wife and has fits of jealousy for no reason.

MEINHARD: Right, she's in her sixth or seventh month now and running around with that big belly, and he acts as if she's carrying on with other men.

Meinhard has finished transferring the honey and wipes the last bits out of the jar with his finger and licks it.

130. Same as 98. The family portrait on the wall. Rigid poses.

Inner Courtyard of the Fortress

131. Becker and Meinhard are sitting in the courtyard on large blocks of stone, surrounded by cardboard tubes, string, shredded wool, and several tin containers with powder in them. They are fabricating fireworks, as one can see from several finished tubes mounted on wooden sticks that have been stuck into the ground. The camera travels to the cottage, where Stroszek is coming out to join the others.

STROSZEK: All right, I'm ready to help again. I see you've been working hard.

MEINHARD: We've finished ten already.

132. Close-up. Becker ties a string around a tube he has just filled with powder, knots the string, and bites off the loose ends. He speaks from between his teeth.

BECKER: And these'll definitely work. We mixed in some sawdust and loose wool. That'll keep them from exploding all at once.

133. From the side. All three are throwing themselves into the work. Meinhard gathers up the finished rockets and lays them out neatly side by side.

STROSZEK: The ones we made yesterday weren't much good. Real duds. Like firecrackers.

MEINHARD: With the sawdust the fire comes out the back nice and even.

134. Close-up. Several rockets side by side that have already been attached to wooden sticks and provided with a fuse.

135. Medium long shot. The men keep on filling the tubes.

STROSZEK: Do you think the colonel will let us shoot them off?

MEINHARD: Well, if it's a boy, I'm sure he'll allow it. And for a daughter, the same. But we've got plenty of time.

BECKER: Let's try one out, though.

STROSZEK: Good.

136. Close-up. They get ready to wedge one of the rockets between two stones.

STROSZEK: Oh, wait a minute. Let me warn my wife, in case it blows up again.

137. Stroszek heads for the cottage.

138. Close-up. Becker and Meinhard secure the rocket. Becker is still twisting the fuse.

139. Medium long shot. From Becker and Meinhard's point of view. Stroszek comes out of the cottage with Nora.

NORA: I want to see, too. This is exciting.

STROSZEK: All right, but go stand over there so nothing happens to you.

140. Close-up. Meinhard lights the rocket. The fuse glows briefly, and then a column of fire shoots out of the rocket.

NORA: Bravo, very good!

STROSZEK: It had to work eventually. But the best part is still missing. The fiery shells on top that come down separately.

BECKER: That's going to be the hardest, believe me.

141. Tight close-up. A cicada has fastened itself to the fissured bark of an olive tree. It looks somewhat like our crickets. But what we see is only the shell, which it left behind. The cicada departed from its existence through its back, where a split can be seen, leaving behind its glassy transparent form, with even the most delicate feelers hollow.

Wall of the Fortress

142. Stroszek is on top of the wall, sitting in one of the cannon loopholes that look out over the ocean on the side of the fortress

that faces away from the town. Boiling midday heat. A slight rustling from the ocean, which comes up almost to the base of the fortress. Stroszek is smoking.

143. Close-up. Stroszek sits up straighter and peers attentively over the wall.

STROSZEK: Why don't you roll your pants up?

144. Camera from Stroszek's point of view, as he peers down from the wall. A level strip of sand about ten meters wide runs along the base of the wall here, and on the other side is the open sea. Down below Meinhard is groping his way barefoot among the wavelets that wash up onshore, but then he returns to the dry sand and sits down to roll up his pant legs. He has two bottles with him. The camera travels to the right, scanning the strip of sand. At some distance are four children.

Beach below the Fortress

145. Close-up. Meinhard is sitting on the sand, his pants rolled up to his knees. He takes the two bottles and digs a piece of bread and a roll of twine out of his pocket.

146. Long shot. From Meinhard's point of view. In the background the four children are huddled around a cardboard box.

147. Same as 145. Meinhard pushes small chunks of bread into the bottles, then fastens twine to the bottles' necks, gets up, and fills the bottles with water, in which we see the bread swimming around.

148. Pan up the wall. Stroszek looks down in the direction of the children.

STROSZEK: Take a look over there. They've got a rooster.

149. Meinhard, who's about to toss a bottle into the ocean, turns to look.

150. Long shot. The long strip of sand and the wall of the fortress. In the background the children have lifted the large rooster they caught out of the box and are holding it to the ground.

151. Somewhat closer. It's clear that none of the children is older than six. The smallest one, who's completely naked, can't be more than three. But he's not afraid of the rooster, which is pecking frantically in all directions.

152. Medium long shot. The strongest child struggles to hold down the rooster as it tries desperately to defend itself, while the other three children attempt to twist its neck, at which they don't succeed because they can't get a good grip on the neck. Then they look for a largish rock but find none on the sand.

153. Close-up. The children force the rooster back into the box, and while one of them holds the top closed the others hastily begin to dig a hole in the sand with their hands, planning to bury the rooster.

154. They place the box in the hole, but it's too shallow. They continue digging until the hole is about half a meter deep.

155. Meinhard is still standing by the water and calls up to Stroszek.

MEINHARD: Do you think they mean to roast him?

156. Stroszek on the wall.

STROSZEK: It doesn't look that way. They don't have anything to build a fire with.

157. Close-up. The children place the box in the hole and throw the sand they dug out on top, forming a small mound. The children back away a short distance and sit down by the wall in a tight cluster. They wait.

158. Meinhard pitches the two bottles, one after the other, about ten meters into the sea, but keeps hold of the ends of the twine so as to be able to pull them out. Then he wraps the ends around two small rocks and leaves them on the sand.

159. Stroszek on the wall. He tosses down a cigarette butt.

STROSZEK: You're not going to catch anything.

160. The children waiting.

MEINHARD'S VOICE: You want to bet? By evening there'll be at least three.

STROSZEK: (Laughs.)

161. Close-up: Meinhard from the front. He's sitting in the sand, pulling a sock onto his wet foot, but notices that there's damp sand clinging to his sole and pulls the sock off.

MEINHARD: I'm coming up now. I'm going to die if I don't get something to drink.

He gets up and holding his shoes in his hand walks along the wall (toward the left). The camera follows him for a while.

162. Medium long shot. In the opposite direction the children huddle together. One of them kneels by the mound of sand, scrapes some away, and puts his ear to the mound. The others approach impatiently and begin hastily to dig out the box.

163. Close-up. The children pull the box halfway out of the sand. One of them lifts the lid impetuously, and the rooster leaps angrily out of the box and escapes. The children are so taken by surprise that they don't run after him as he flees along the beach.

164. Same as 117. The wall of the fortress into which an ancient statue is incorporated as filler, with only the soles of the feet showing.

Kos, the Harbor

165. Long shot. The harbor drive with the fortress in the background; freighters and fishing boats tied up in the harbor. Music from a tavern. With the midday sun beating down, few people to be seen.

166. Two sailors sleeping on grain sacks that have been piled under an awning on the deck of a boat.

167. Men playing a board game in a tavern.

Courtyard of the Fortress

168. Long shot. From the battlements atop the wall. Nothing is stirring. Annoying buzzing of flies in the heat.

169. Medium long shot. The goat, staked near the wall. She stops grazing and remains motionless, keeping close to the wall in its shadow, her head lowered.

170. Meinhard is lying apathetically on the bench by the shed next to the cottage. His labored breathing reveals the oppressive effect the heat is having on him (camera lingers). After a while he slowly wipes the beads of sweat from his upper lip.

171. Becker is sitting on the battlements with his legs dangling over the wall. He has a white undershirt draped over his head.

172. Close-up. His right hand plays languidly with a *konvoloi,* a rosary-like string of beads customarily used by the natives.

Kos, the Harbor

173. An old fisherman who has caught an octopus rhythmically pounds it on a stone by the pier to tenderize it for cooking.

Kos, the Marketplace

174. Long shot. The square marketplace on the inner part of town. A broad space bordered by houses with arcades; much activity. Market stalls, coffeehouse chairs set out far into the square, much shouting. On one side a very small mosque from the days of the Turkish occupation is still standing, with a shade tree and a fountain for foot washing in front. The camera pans over the square.

175. One of the market stalls with fruit on its counters, a dense layer of wasps hovering over it. The vendor gesticulating vigorously, trying time after time to drive away the wasps with a folded-up newspaper.

176. Medium long shot. A group of farmers unloading their pack donkeys. Stroszek strolls into the square. The camera travels in front of him until he stops at one of the fruit stands.

Kos, Narrow Street

177. A narrow, quiet street. At its end a large mosque, complete with a tall minaret. Women and girls sit in front of the houses chatting.

178. Stroszek turns onto the street. The camera travels beside him. The women observe him with unconcealed curiosity.

179. From the front. Stroszek has reached the mosque, in front of which stands a rickety truck. From external changes to the structure one can see that the mosque is being used in part as a dwelling and a warehouse. Several emaciated cats are prowling about.

180. An old woman sits by the entrance to an addition to the mosque. Stroszek goes up to her. Soft piano music mixes with the street sounds.

STROSZEK (in Greek): Good day.

WOMAN (in Greek): Good day.

STROSZEK (in Greek): Excuse me, may I take a look inside?

WOMAN (in Greek): Certainly. Come with me.

STROSZEK (in Greek): So, are there no more Turks here, no Muslims?

WOMAN (in Greek): Oh, no. The last of them left, ah, forty years ago . . . . We have to go through the kitchen.

Kos, Inside the Mosque

181. Camera in a small kitchen area, outfitted simply. The door opens and the woman leads Stroszek in. The camera pans with them. The woman opens a very low door on one side—the original entrance to the mosque. She lets Stroszek go ahead; he has to stoop to get through the doorway. Loud piano music from the interior.

182. Long shot. The main hall of the mosque. Between the slim columns on the left, old petroleum barrels are stacked almost to the ceiling. In the middle, straggling rows of chairs under a high dome. At the front a battered piano stands on a small platform. A young soldier is playing.

183. Close-up. The old woman, standing in the doorway, points at the soldier.

WOMAN (in Greek): He's one of yours. He's almost always here.

184. Stroszek approaches the piano rather hesitantly, so as not to disturb the player. But the pianist has stopped playing as soon as Stroszek entered and turns to the new arrival.

PIANIST: Come here; I don't mind.

STROSZEK: I wouldn't have expected to find one of us here.

185. Close-up from the side. The pianist has stood up and pulled up a chair for Stroszek. Both men sit down.

STROSZEK: Thank you.

PIANIST: I get to play here almost every day. At least in the morn-
ings; that's when it's easiest to get off duty . . . . Aren't you part
of the munitions depot detail, sir?

STROSZEK: No need to be formal.

PIANIST: Fine by me. Is it true that one of you was allowed to marry
and has his wife with him?

STROSZEK: That's me.

PIANIST: You don't say! Well, congratulations. Listen, I'm going
to finish this piece, and then I'll show you the minaret and the
domes.

STROSZEK: I don't know a thing about music. What are you playing?

PIANIST: It's a Chopin sonata. In F major.

The pianist turns to the piano and plays with deep emotion.
Stroszek listens politely but without much interest. His gaze roves
through the space. The camera lingers.

On the Roof of the Mosque

186. Blindingly bright sky. From the roof one can look down at
the narrow, dark opening at the base of the minaret that leads to
the section of the roof with the domes. The pianist and Stroszek
squeeze through the opening, feeling dizzy and dazed by the light.

STROSZEK: I'm dizzy from that spiral staircase. Going up into the
tower was all right, but then coming down here to the roof
makes your head spin.

PIANIST: You get used to it.

187. View from the roof over the mosque's dazzlingly white
domes. The roofs of the town, with the sea and the fortress in the
background.

188. Medium long shot. Stroszek goes over to the first white-washed dome and tries to scramble up it but promptly slides back down. The pianist sits down on a low ledge.

PIANIST: This is my favorite place. No one comes up here, and you can see everything. The whole town and the sea and the rest of the island on the other side.

STROSZEK: But the light's pretty blinding. It'd be better to come here in the evening or at night.

PIANIST: Do you feel it too? The sense of being sheltered here. Especially down below in the mosque. I don't know why. It's always nice and cool; the Turks knew how to build for that better than anyone.

189. View from the roof into a nearby courtyard. The entire house, with hardly any windows on the street side, is oriented toward the walled courtyard: all the windows face in that direction. Turkish-style garden, cats on the roof.

190. Stroszek is leaning at an angle against the dome.

STROSZEK: Yes, this is a good place. But it would be too lonely for me.

PIANIST: That's why I play the piano.

Inside the Mosque

191. Close-up. The soldier at the piano. Stroszek has moved his chair very close and is listening to him play. After a while the pianist suddenly stops playing.

STROSZEK: That was lovely.

PIANIST: I wanted to show you something: Chopin is almost always played wrong. The runs . . . (he plays a run with his right hand) . . . shouldn't be played this way. There should be continuity, but . . .

STROSZEK: I wouldn't be able to tell the difference.

PIANIST: . . . but every note should be distinct; it should sound like a string of bubbles.

He plays the run again.

STROSZEK: It sounds almost the same. I don't get the point you're making.

192. Same as 102. The damaged ancient marble statue. Stern posture, weathered face, blank eyes.

Kos, Outside the Military Headquarters

193. The occupation unit's headquarters are located on the harbor drive. An outdoor flight of whitewashed stone steps leads to the commandant's office. Outside the door, above which a sign is posted, stands an armed guard. Stroszek mounts the steps.

194. Stroszek from close up. He salutes the guard.

Inside the Headquarters

195. A colonel is sitting behind his desk in a room provisionally set up as an office. He flips inattentively through a file. Behind him on the wall is a general-staff map.

196. Medium long shot. Stroszek enters through the open door and stands at attention. The camera moves behind him to show both him and the colonel.

COLONEL: So, how's it going?

STROSZEK: Stroszek reporting, Sir: no particular incidents.

The colonel gets up and comes from behind his desk toward Stroszek.

197. Close-up. The colonel and Stroszek.

COLONEL: And otherwise . . . I mean, are you experiencing any difficulties?

STROSZEK: No . . . no, not really.

COLONEL: Feel free to say so if you're having any problems.

STROSZEK: Everything is all right, really. We're all getting along, except . . . how should I put it? All of us spent a lot of time in sick bay, and in the fortress we don't get much exercise either.

COLONEL: Would you like us to assign you to reconnaissance patrols now and then?

STROSZEK: Yes, that would certainly do us good.

COLONEL: All right, listen: tomorrow I'll send you up to the ridge in the southeast. There's no threat, but we need to make our presence known there again. Take Meinhard with you.

STROSZEK: Pardon me, but I think his meniscus isn't completely healed yet.

COLONEL: All right, then take Becker. I'll show you on the map where it is.

198. Close-up. The colonel and Stroszek looking at the map.

COLONEL: First stay far to the east in Sector 2. Then along here to the ridgeline. You can return sometime in late afternoon.

STROSZEK: Yes, Sir.

COLONEL: Report to me when you get back. All right then, good luck. And say hello to your wife for me.

STROSZEK: Thank you.

199. Same as 53. Narrow, silvery olive tree leaves stirring slightly in the breeze.

Courtyard of the Fortress

200. Becker has dismantled his gun on a block of stone near the shed and is cleaning the parts with oil rags. To his left Stroszek and Meinhard are moving the stake to which the goat is attached.

STROSZEK: We should move her more often. She eats everything down to the roots where she's staked, and then she has nothing left.

BECKER: But put her more over there so she has some shade.

MEINHARD: You two better hurry, otherwise you'll get caught in the midday heat . . . . Do you think from the ridgeline you'll be able to see across to the sea on the other side?

BECKER: The island's fairly narrow. But you can never be sure. Maybe there are other mountains beyond these.

Kos, Open Landscape

201. Long shot (wide angle). View from the edge of town. First, fields and olive trees. Behind them a chain of mountains rises, stretching the length of the island. Slight pan. The morning sun falls at an angle that picks out the jagged, broken profiles of the mountain chain. Treeless heights, karst formations. Chirping of cicadas in the morning heat. A donkey brays.

202. Stroszek and Becker come toward the camera from the edge of town, following a stone wall. Both are armed.

203. From the side. The two men follow a cart track. Rocky, barren fields, thistles, agaves, and fig trees. The camera travels alongside them.

204. Stroszek and Becker from a higher vantage point (long focal-length lens). They've already reached the base of the mountain range and are climbing on a zigzag course. Several times Becker leans on his rifle stock. They seem to be making hardly any headway (because of the long focal length). The camera lingers.

205. Close-up. From behind. Their feet slowly climbing past clumps of thorny vegetation.

206. Medium long shot. From the front, at an angle. Stroszek is ahead of Becker, whose face is dripping with sweat. In the meantime the landscape has become treeless and rocky. The only vegetation is the thorny clumps, low to the ground.

BECKER: Do you have anything left to drink?

STROSZEK: No. We didn't take nearly enough with us.

BECKER: Then we should definitely head for that house up there.

STROSZEK: It's still pretty far.

207. View of the mountainside above them. Fairly far up, still several hundred meters away, is a very squat house, whitewashed.

208. Same as 205. The feet of the two men toiling up the mountain.

209. The two from behind. They're already quite close to the house. A shepherd comes out of the door and stands calmly by the low wall of his front courtyard, waiting for the men as they approach.

210. The shepherd, close up. He is lean and sinewy, with well-defined facial features. He stands there motionless.

211. Stroszek and Becker have come to within five meters.

STROSZEK: (in Greek): Good day.

SHEPHERD (in Greek): Good day.

Stroszek removes his gun from his shoulder and turns to Becker.

STROSZEK: Let's leave the guns outside. It's better that way.

Becker hesitates at first, but then, like Stroszek, leans his gun against the outside of the stone wall surrounding the courtyard. Then they enter.

212. From the house. The small front courtyard with a well in the middle. The shepherd hands the men a pail of water and a tin drinking cup. Then he calls in a rather peremptory tone into the house.

213. The house. It has a very low ceiling and only one window opening. The door is open into the dark interior, and on the threshold lies the head of a recently slaughtered ram, next to which all four legs are neatly lined up. A woman and a shy, rather wild-looking little girl come outside and greet the men.

214. Close-up. The shepherd urges his guests to sit on a bench near the house by a rough-hewn table.

STROSZEK: (in Greek): Please don't go to too much trouble.

The shepherd gives the girl an order. She runs to the outer wall of the courtyard and drags back the two guns. The camera pans with her. The girl leans the guns against the wall of the house, close to the door.

BECKER: Look, she brought us our guns.

STROSZEK (in Greek): Thank you very much.

215. The woman comes out of the house and places heaping plates before the men.

BECKER: If we eat all that, our stomachs will explode.

STROSZEK: Yes, but we have to eat it, no matter what.

They eat for a while, making it clear that they are enjoying the food.

216. Close-up. The wall of the house with the two guns leaning against it. To the left of that spot the dark doorway with the bloody ram's head and the legs on the threshold.

217. From the side. The shepherd, who is sitting across from Becker, pushes a handful of oil-cured olives over to him. The plates are already empty. Becker gestures that he's had his fill but then takes a few olives to be polite.

BECKER: This is more work than climbing up here.

STROSZEK: We should be pushing on soon . . . . Wait, I have a picture postcard from home—I'll give it to him. Other than that, I don't have anything I could offer him.

He pulls a postcard out of his breast pocket and gives it to the shepherd.

STROSZEK (in Greek): This is for you. I'm sorry I don't have anything else. That's a picture of the big church in my hometown.

The shepherd proudly takes the postcard and summons his wife and daughter to look.

SHEPHERD (in Greek): Look, that's the big church in his hometown. Agapi, sing them that song you learned in school.

218. Close-up. The shepherd addresses Stroszek.

SHEPHERD (in Greek): She's going to sing you a song she learned in school. She's in second grade already and has to go down to town every day. Sometimes she spends the night with her aunt, so she'll get to be among people. When she started school, she could hardly speak because it's so lonely up here. It really worries me that she has so little chance to speak . . . . Go ahead and sing it to them—they won't hurt you.

The camera pans to the girl, who is standing in the doorway looking quite intimidated. The ram's head and legs are still on the threshold. She sings:

GIRL (in Greek):   High up on Lasithi Mountain
                   Ninety-two lambs graze.
                   One fell into the Tyrnavos Gorge
                   Before dawn.
                   Hurry, shepherds, hurry:
                   Above the Tyrnavos Gorge
                   Vultures are circling.

219. Long shot. Stroszek and Becker have left the house and are climbing again, quite high by now. Midday heat.

220. The camera is focused forward at an angle on the jagged, rocky ground and pans up the mountainside.

221. Same as 205. The feet of the two men climbing.

222. Medium close-up. From the front, at an angle. Stroszek in the lead, his expression abstracted, while Becker toils along behind.

BECKER: We should almost be there. The ridge must be up by that gap.

223. All sounds fall silent (footsteps, cicadas' chirping). The camera approaches a small gap at the mountaintop. The ridge wobbles from the men's movements. Sudden halt. All at once one can see the sea on the other side. On the horizon toward the Turkish coast, farther to the right and looking like filmy clouds hovering over the ocean in the haze, the islands near Rhodes. In the silence, a scream from Stroszek.

224. Frontal view. Stroszek is screaming in a sudden fit of insanity, his voice cracking. He points in the direction of the islands and scoops up rocks from the ground. Becker is incredulous.

225. Screeching, Stroszek hurls the rocks at the islands. The closest one is 30 kilometers away. He is foaming at the mouth. He raises his hand with the last rock, then lets it drop and pulls his gun off his shoulder.

226. From behind. Stroszek aims and fires in the direction of the islands. Becker jumps him from the right and tries to grab his gun. The two men tumble over backward. Stroszek fires as he falls and continues firing from the ground.

227. Close-up. Stroszek screams and continues firing. Becker rolls away to the side to avoid being hit.

228. Becker runs off. The camera pans with him. Sudden silence. The camera pans back to Stroszek, who has emptied his magazine from his position on the ground. He is panting and lowers his gun.

229. Long shot. From Stroszek's point of view. The calm sea, almost as flat as a mirror. The islands light and hazy, seeming to float. Not a cloud in the sky.

230. Becker cautiously approaches Stroszek, still lying on the ground but by now quite a bit calmer.

BECKER: Come, let's go down to the house . . . to people.

STROSZEK: What just happened? . . . I mustn't forget my gun.

Stroszek gets up slowly, coming to his senses. Becker helps him up and leads him away, guiding him by the elbow. Stroszek complies like a child.

231. Same as 141. The hollow, transparent exoskeleton of a cicada on the bark of an olive tree.

The Fortress, Inside the Cottage

232. The back room. The three men of the detail are at the table having lunch. They've almost finished. Nora removes two serving dishes, her movements tense and hasty. All of them are feeling the unnatural atmosphere, as their movements and the looks they exchange reveal. Stroszek is treated with excessive solicitude; he notices and reacts with suspicion. Nora pours wine for him, but only half a glass, and then dilutes it with water. She hands it to him with forced cheerfulness.

NORA: Here, drink, is good in this heat.

STROSZEK: You know I don't like this swill . . . . What? Why are you all looking at me like that?

Nora cringes and takes the glass away at once.

233. Close-up of Stroszek. He eats, keeping a hypervigilant eye on the others. No one says a word. The clatter of the knives and forks is irritating.

234. The table from Stroszek's point of view. The two other soldiers eat with apparent casualness. But Meinhard gets his knife and fork mixed up. Nora takes something back to the kitchen again.

235. The camera pans over two walls of the room. A window, Stroszek's gun, and an icon.

236. Meinhard turns to Becker and puts down his fork.

MEINHARD: Today at five we're supposed to report to the company doctor for a check-up.

STROSZEK: How come? We're only supposed to go every two weeks.

BECKER: I have no idea. They do whatever occurs to them. But I think they mean to send you home on the next transport, or so I heard.

Stroszek gives a strange laugh.

STROSZEK: Me? Why me? . . . Because of yesterday on the mountain? Did you report me? You said you weren't going to say anything.

Becker remains silent and doesn't answer Stroszek's question. Stroszek leaps to his feet like an animal.

STROSZEK: Did you sell me out?

237. Close-up. Meinhard gets up and urges him reassuringly to sit down.

MEINHARD: Look, it's all going to be for the best. Nora and he went to the colonel this morning, and he promised . . .

Stroszek is about to attack Nora, but Meinhard gets between them, and Becker also comes to her defense.

STROSZEK: You told on me, you bitch! The colonel! I knew something was going on between her and the colonel.

He breaks free from Meinhard.

STROSZEK: Keep your hands off me! . . . She wants to get rid of me,
    the bitch, so she and the colonel . . .

Becker and Meinhard grab Stroszek as he tries to get at Nora
again. That makes him even more crazed.

STROSZEK: Take your hands off me!

238. Medium long shot. As Becker and Meinhard try to force him
back onto his seat, he suddenly pulls free and knocks the whole
table over. The camera pans along. Stroszek dashes to the corner
and grabs his gun, which he promptly aims at the other men. They
freeze for a moment, unsure as to what to do. Nora weeps silently.

STROSZEK: Get out! . . . Get the hell out!

Becker is dismayed and takes a few steps back. Meinhard hesitates, but then cautiously steps forward to knock the gun out of
Stroszek's hands. At that Stroszek fires into the wall, just missing him.

BECKER: Do what he says.

They both get out of the way, Becker pushing Nora ahead of him.
She's paralyzed with fear.

Kos, the Harbor
239. Long shot. The harbor drive, normal activity. Two ships are
just being unloaded. Workmen are carrying baskets full of fish
out of one and melons out of another, passing the melons along a
chain of men to a nearby truck. Bystanders, the two boys fishing,
the fisherman with his nets spread around him.

Courtyard of the Fortress
240. The exterior of the cottage. The three back out of the door,
followed closely by Stroszek, pointing his gun at them.

241. Long shot. From the battlements atop the wall. Driven by Stroszek, the three hastily turn toward the gate and break into a run.

Kos, the Harbor

242. Close-up. The fisherman among his nets (see 75). He's just lighting a cigarette, which he had tucked behind his ear. Suddenly shots are heard.

243. Same as 239. Activity along the harbor drive. Only after a second or two do the people there pause in their work. A melon rolls to the ground.

A VOICE (in Greek): They're shooting at us!

The people flee across the road to the buildings.

244. Close-up. The two boys fishing. One of them jumps up and runs away while the other one quickly hauls in his line and then takes to his heels.

245. Long shot. Pan across the empty harbor drive. Isolated shots ring out as the camera continues to pan. Near the boats the fisherman is still sitting as though nothing were amiss. In the middle of the road lies a donkey that's been hit.

246. The fisherman close up. He has the net stretched between his two big toes and is mending it. He doesn't remove his cigarette because he has no hand free.

247. View of the fortress from the harbor drive. No movement to be seen. The shots are coming from one of the loopholes.

248. Medium long shot. The entrance to one of the houses in which several people have sought refuge. A man calls to the outside.

MAN (in Greek): Come inside, Christos. They're going to hit you.

249. Same as 246. The fisherman spits out his half-smoked cigarette and laughs.

250. One of the ships has a completely desiccated octopus hanging from its mast. No purpose is apparent.

Inside the Headquarters

251. The commandant's office. Feverish activity. Three soldiers
are barricading the windows with sandbags. The colonel is standing agitatedly behind his desk and speaking on the telephone.
Gunshots can be heard.

COLONEL: Yes, at the depot. It must be partisans. Yes . . . yes . . . .
 Block the bypass immediately and Palamidius Street . . . park
 trucks across them, yes, forthwith . . . nothing to see, the shots
 presumably coming from houses in the area . . . wait a moment.

252. From the desk. Becker and Meinhard rush into the room and
stand at attention. Nora behind them.

BECKER: Colonel, Sir, Stroszek has lost his mind!

COLONEL: What?

MEINHARD: Yes, he was firing at us from behind.

COLONEL: Pull yourself together. What happened?

BECKER: It was just like yesterday. Suddenly he started raving and
 threatened us with his gun.

COLONEL: Why didn't you disarm him?

MEINHARD: It was impossible. He fired right past me. He would've
 mowed us all down.

253. The colonel, close up. He picks up the receiver again.

COLONEL: Hello? Are you still there? It's not partisans. One member of the fortress detail has gone crazy and is shooting in all
 directions . . . . Yes, maintain state of alert . . . . No street block-

ages, pull back the special unit . . . . Yes, send reinforcements
. . . . Good, talk to you later.

254. From the doorway. The colonel sinks onto his chair. The soldiers with the sandbags and the group from the fortress stand there uncertainly.

COLONEL: We'll get this under control. We should've been more
   careful from the start . . . . Has he barricaded himself inside?

MEINHARD: He locked the gate. But that was all we had a chance to
   see.

NORA: Please, let me go back. I can get my husband. He listen
   to me.

COLONEL: I had that same thought. But right now it's too
   dangerous. For the present we'll wait and observe him until he
   calms down. Maybe he'll come out on his own then. But you
   absolutely mustn't go now. I'm having some reinforcements sent.

Kos, the Harbor

255. Long shot. The deserted harbor drive with the fortress in the background. The gunshots have stopped. But Stroszek can be heard shouting unintelligibly.

256. The entrance to the commandant's office, located on the harbor drive. The colonel comes to the door from inside and looks at the fortress through heavy-duty binoculars. Behind him Meinhard and another soldier come into view.

257. Close-up. The colonel puts down his binoculars.

COLONEL: If this continues, we'll have to move our headquarters.
   The approach is too dangerous . . . . Come with me. But keep
   close to the wall and turn left at the corner.

258. From the middle of the street. At short intervals Becker, Nora, three other soldiers, Meinhard, and finally the colonel run

down the steps, dash along the wall of the building, and at the corner turn left onto the next side street. They make it without incident. Only shouts coming from the fortress.

259. On the side street. Heavily armed soldiers climb out of a truck and line up in formation. In front of them, in a Jeep that has stopped close to where the side street meets the harbor drive, a lieutenant, who is standing up in the vehicle, observing the fortress through his binoculars. The doorways are crowded with residents of the town who seem more curious than fearful. The colonel rounds the corner after the others from his office and salutes the lieutenant.

260. The colonel and the lieutenant from close up.

COLONEL: First, post guards. But unobtrusively, so as not to rile him . . . . I'm hoping that in an hour or two we can use his wife's help to get him to come out.

261. Same as 36. A wall into which an ancient piece of marble has been incorporated, with a well-preserved frieze.

262. View of the deserted harbor drive and the fortress. Only Christos the fisherman is still there among his nets. Some melons that were dropped on the ground. The dead donkey in the middle of the road.

263. A house along the harbor drive. In an upper window stands a sentry with binoculars. The shutters of the other windows are all closed.

264. The far side of the fortress. The narrow strip of sand that runs along the base of the wall continues along a breakwater beyond the harbor (i.e., the breakwater protects a road along the shore and several houses outside the town limits). A couple of two-wheeled carts stand there, behind which a sentry has taken cover.

265. The sentry from close up. He stands motionless.

266. A further sentry at the lighthouse near the mouth of the harbor, across from the fortress. Nothing stirring.

267. Long shot. The harbor drive. Nora walking toward the fortress. Four soldiers follow her, among them Meinhard. They hug the walls of the houses.

268. Same as 265. A motionless sentry.

269. The camera travels in front of the group. The lieutenant is leading the soldiers. Nora is far ahead, her movements more anxious than determined.

270. The group from behind. They're just passing two fishing cutters that have been drawn up on land and rest on wooden rollers on a level spot by the harbor, with the fortress almost looming over them. They are covered with rust. The camera pans slightly upward to where Stroszek appears in one of the loopholes widened for a cannon, holding his gun. All the soldiers come to a halt; only Nora advances a few more steps.

271. Stroszek, perhaps from Nora's point of view. The wall of the fortress is a good 10 meters high, with Stroszek standing up above in a menacing posture.

272. Nora from close up. She speaks as if to a sick child.

NORA: Come down to us; you not need to be afraid. All is good
again.

Stroszek (off screen) begins to laugh crazily.

273. Stroszek up on the wall.

STROSZEK: Get away from there, you . . . you. This minute.

He takes a step backward in a threatening manner.

274. Nora from close up.

NORA: Come down here, please, please!

STROSZEK'S VOICE: Beat it, you sons of bitches!

The lieutenant joins the exchange as the camera pans to him. He speaks very sharply.

LIEUTENANT: Stroszek! Come down here this minute! That's an order.

275. Stroszek fires a shot without aiming and at the same time jumps back. Rapid pan to the group of soldiers, who take cover behind the fishing boats nearby. Nora reacts somewhat more slowly, running off down the harbor drive completely unprotected.

MEINHARD'S VOICE: Nora! Take cover!

276. Close-up. The four soldiers on the ground behind the boats.

LIEUTENANT: Fire! He mustn't have a chance to shoot or he'll hit his wife.

They fire in rapid succession to force Stroszek to take cover. Stroszek can be heard shouting unintelligibly, then more clearly.

STROSZEK'S VOICE: Stop it, you sons of bitches! I'll blow you all sky-high. I'll blow everything sky-high, all the munitions.

MEINHARD: My god, he's going to blow up the entire munitions depot.

LIEUTENANT: Hold your fire!

MEINHARD: All he needs to do is toss a grenade in there. We can't get in fast enough. Half the town will go up.

LIEUTENANT: Damn! We have to pull back; otherwise he's crazy enough to do it.

277. Long shot. The soldiers begin to retreat, using all available cover. In the background the fortress, from which Stroszek's voice can be heard.

STROSZEK'S VOICE: Giving me orders . . . (he laughs hysterically)
   me . . . . I'm the commander and you're nothing but shit.

278. Same as 117. Wall of the fortress, into which an ancient statue
has been incorporated in such a way that only the soles of the
feet show.

Inside the New Headquarters

279. A large emptied-out room with several windows. Along the
front wall a long table at which seven people are seated. The colonel, the lieutenant, Becker, Meinhard, a company doctor, and two
Greeks. One of them, a hulking but very agile middle-aged man,
and next to him the town elder. Several military maps lie on the
table.

COLONEL: That was a mistake. We should have moved decisively
   right away. Now he's even more crazed and won't let his guard
   down. We can't get sharpshooters close enough without running
   the risk that he may see them and blow up the depot.

He stands up, lights a cigarette, and strides back and forth.

COLONEL: What do you think, Doctor? Is there any chance he might
   go back to normal?

280. The doctor from close up.

COMPANY DOCTOR: At the moment I have very few records to go
   on, unfortunately. Most importantly, the initial hospital reports
   on the precise nature of his injury are missing. But as far as it's
   possible to guess, his condition might return to normal as it did
   yesterday, briefly, after his first attack. Which is not to say that
   normalization will come quickly, if at all. The factors are very
   complicated . . .

COLONEL: How should we proceed?

COMPANY DOCTOR: Very cautiously, no matter what. In a case like
   this the patient is usually in a state of heightened irritability, but
   in spite of his disturbed mental balance he is certainly capable

of acting logically and intelligently. That he may blow up the depot—if he feels provoked into doing so—is certainly within the realm of possibility from a medical perspective.

COLONEL: And from a technical perspective? Becker, does he have the technical ability to do that?

BECKER: I'm afraid he does. He has the key to the depot. And if he's made preparations, it can happen fast. It could be ignited with a bunch of hand grenades, maybe also with an electrical cable from the lighting system . . .

COLONEL: Then we'll shut off the current immediately.

MEINHARD: Pardon me. He has another method that's even more of a sure thing. There's gasoline in the fortress. If he dumps it out and drops a match into it, that's it.

COLONEL: How much explosive power do the munitions have?

LIEUTENANT: We're not quite finished with the calculations. But a preliminary estimate would be, let's say, about five to six tonnes of TNT. If all the underwater mines explode, that is. The ammunition is less dangerous, so it seems.

COLONEL: But that's enough to put parts of the town at risk.

LIEUTENANT: Yes, that's true. But it's not the case that half the town would be blown up. The destruction in the fortress would be so great, however, that at least the nearby houses would be affected. Primarily by stones crashing down on them.

COLONEL: That forces us to evacuate nearby buildings . . . . Herr Vassiliou, we've included you in this meeting as a representative of the civilian population. You see that this measure is necessary, and also what you would want. Do you understand what I'm saying?

VASSILIOU: Yes, of course. I spent three years at the university in Germany . . . . It's hard to get people to leave their homes. We also don't have other houses in which to put them up. So many have German soldiers billeted in them.

The town elder sitting next to him turns to Vassiliou and speaks quietly to him.

VASSILIOU: Excuse me, he's asking whether something can't be done soon. He says there isn't much left to eat, and it's not possible to unload the ships. The ships can't leave the harbor, either.

COLONEL: At the moment there's nothing we can do. At most, after dark. Today the risk is still too great. If he remains quiet, we'll wait through the night. Tomorrow he'll be back to normal, and if not, tomorrow night he'll certainly fall asleep, or at least let down his guard. Then we can go in. Herr Vassiliou, we'll have to discuss the measures for a temporary evacuation with you separately. Probably those affected will have to leave their household goods behind to make the operation as simple as possible.

281. Same as 250. A completely desiccated octopus hangs from the mast of a ship.

Kos, the Harbor

282. Long shot. The abandoned harbor drive. Even Christos the fisherman has been forced to go into hiding. Only a few dogs and the dead donkey remain. No sounds but Stroszek's voice in the background, coming from the fortress.

STROSZEK'S VOICE: Don't think you're ever going to get in here, you sons of bitches . . .

283. One of the houses along the harbor drive, close to the fortress, with closed shutters. The camera pans along the façade as far as the corner, which allows one to see into the side street. People are climbing out of a ground-floor window onto the street.

STROSZEK'S VOICE: . . . not in three weeks and not in three years . . .

284. On the side street. Close to the people. They are two older women and a man who helps them from inside as they scramble over the window ledge. From outside a German soldier lends them a hand. The two women accept the awkwardness with dignity.

STROSZEK'S VOICE: . . . I can catch trout with my bare hands—could
   from the time I was a boy . . .

285. From inside the man passes out a fairly large bundle of bedding, and he's about to fetch other household items, but the soldier
stops him.

STROSZEK'S VOICE: . . . when I was only ten. You were still pooping
   in your pants . . .

286. The camera travels to the window. The man leaves his possessions behind, regretfully, but bends over one more time and
picks up three pictures.

STROSZEK'S VOICE: . . . (hysterical laughter) I'm the
   commandant . . .

287. Medium long shot. The man finds it hard to climb out of
the window with the pictures under his arm. One of the women
takes them from him and leans them against the outside wall for
the moment.

STROSZEK'S VOICE: . . . If you come, I'm going to blow this whole
   place in the air. Don't think you'll catch me sleeping . . .

288. The pictures from close up. One is about 70 by 30 centime-
ters, framed with glass, a popular cheap print showing a mild-
looking Christ with long curls standing on Mount Olive in the
moonlight. Leaning on top of that one and partially covering it,
a family portrait. The man in the photo has a gun and a wide ammunition belt. To the right of these two pictures a small, smoke-
darkened icon.

STROSZEK'S VOICE: . . . I can tell which direction you're coming
   from, I can smell it . . .

Courtyard of a House

289. The back door of a house that opens onto a small walled courtyard, part of which is shaded by a pergola. In the courtyard are a man, a woman, two children, a soldier, and a dog. Bedding is spread on the ground, and the man is rolling it up and wrapping it in a bed sheet. The woman is rushing to water all the plants, while the children hold on to the dog in one corner.

STROSZEK'S VOICE: . . . when it's pitch black and I'm in the woods, I can find my way out blindfolded because I can sense the direction . . .

290. The man lifts the bundle to the top of the wall, and hands reach up from the other side to take it.

STROSZEK'S VOICE: . . . then I'll blow you all sky-high, every single one of you . . .

291. The children want to lift the dog over the wall, but they aren't tall enough. They try to push it by its hindquarters. The soldier steps in and lifts the dog onto the top of the wall. It too is received by the hands on the other side.

STROSZEK'S VOICE: Just show your faces, you fucking cowards. I'll show you . . .

292. The man has fetched a table, which he pushes against the wall. From there the whole family climbs to the other side.

STROSZEK'S VOICE: Show your faces! (His voice cracks; short pause, then two shots ring out.)

Kos, the Harbor

293. One of the side streets. About a dozen evacuees. Soldiers with two-wheeled carts into which the people's possessions are loaded.

294. At some distance. A small procession heading into town.

295. A house façade, the shutters closed.

Inside the New Headquarters

296. The colonel in the new office into which he has moved. It's not fully set up. He paces restlessly, deep in thought. The lieutenant is standing at the end of the table. Outdoors it's already dark.

LIEUTENANT: I checked on it myself. The evacuation has been completed. At the moment sixty-five members of the civilian population are affected.

COLONEL: Did everything go smoothly?

LIEUTENANT: There were no incidents. The population was very cooperative.

COLONEL: And what is Stroszek up to?

LIEUTENANT: As it got dark he became more agitated. Maybe he fears an attack. He's still threatening to blow up the munitions. Also, earlier he appointed himself supreme commander in the eastern Mediterranean.

The colonel is no longer paying attention. Astonished, he interrupts his pacing and hurries over to one of the windows.

COLONEL: What the hell is that?

He opens the window. Flickering lights appear outside.

297. View from the window. Above the houses of the town fireworks can be seen. Rockets shoot into the sky and burst into glowing shells at their zenith.

298. The colonel turns away from the window.

COLONEL: Stroszek! Where did he get those? Come outside with me.

They hurry to the door. The camera pans with them.

Kos, the Harbor

299. Long shot. The harbor drive, nighttime. The streetlights have been turned on, and above them arcs a starry night sky. Lights in the windows of the town. Silence, broken only by a few isolated nocturnal cicadas. From the fortress rockets climb silently into the sky, lighting up everything. The fireworks are somewhat infrequent, appearing at irregular intervals. At their zenith the rockets break into bright fiery spheres that fall slowly and soon burn out. A single rocket flies diagonally, passing low over the roofs of the town.

300. A house. The windows open and people lean out to watch the spectacle.

301. Along the street a scattering of people gathers, gawking in fascination.

302. View of the fortress. The fireworks display reaches its climax. Rockets shoot up in quick succession. The whole sky is lit up. Then the direction changes suddenly, and the sense of playfulness disappears. Several rockets, leaving glowing tails in the silent sky, head directly toward the town, while high in the sky the last fiery shells fade out as they float down. The rockets, fired in quick succession, now travel almost horizontally like tracer munitions straight toward the middle of the town. They take a precise route and come very fast, very close together, very menacingly. They no longer rise to the point where they burst into a cascade of dying flashes. Rapid sequence of rockets.

Suddenly the show breaks off. The fortress lies in darkness again. One becomes conscious of the silence that accompanied the spectacle.

303. Same as 301. The people are still transfixed, fascinated by the violent display.

304. A single streetlight. Around it a moving cloud of mosquitoes. Among them clumsy moths bumping into the lamp.

Kos, the Harbor

305. Long shot. The deserted harbor drive. Only a dog wandering past the houses. Nothing stirring in the fortress.

306. Boats tied up and smallish freighters, almost all equipped additionally with sails, float deserted in the harbor. They rock slightly in the tide.

307. From the harbor drive. View of one of the side streets, where about ten dock workers, barefoot and tanned, with white cloths tied over their heads and hanging down over the backs of their necks, are waiting by an old truck, its engine already running.

308. In the window of a house stands a sentry, scanning the fortress with his binoculars.

309. The sentry at the lighthouse. He too keeps his eyes fixed on the fortress. His elevated position makes it possible for him to see partway into the fortress.

310. Same as 307. Workers waiting on the side street.

311. The sentry at the lighthouse lowers his binoculars and gestures vigorously to the men.

312. The truck starts up slowly, and the dock workers run alongside, using it for cover. The camera pans with them. The truck crosses the harbor drive and comes to a halt beside one of the ships.

313. Medium long shot. The workers begin to unload the ship very hastily. For that purpose, they set a second gangplank in place. They use the first to run onto the deck, and on the second one they

come back onto the dock with large baskets filled with fish. The plank sways under their weight.

314. The truck. On top three men receive the heavy baskets hoisted up to them and stow them on the bed. All the men work quickly, in silence. There's none of the usual laughing and banter.

315. View of the deck, half of which is covered by an awning. The workers come one after the other and lift the baskets already lined up on the deck onto their shoulders.

316. Close-up. One of the baskets. The fish have not been sorted. They have only a dull gleam. Dense swarms of flies hover over them.

317. The gangplanks from the side. Workers hurry onto the ship and return heavily laden. Their steps cause the planks to sway and bend.

318. The sentry at the lighthouse waves emphatically, first with one arm, then with both.

319. Long shot. A shot rings out, then several in quick succession. The workers jump to take cover behind the truck, which quickly starts moving.

320. View of the ship. Two workers have been left behind. They leap into the hold.

321. From the ship. The truck has almost crossed the road. The workers are running alongside, bent double. On the bed one worker has crouched down between two baskets. The truck reaches the safe side of the road.

322. Close-up. Where the truck was parked by the ship, a basket full of fish has been left on the dock.

323. Long shot. View along the harbor drive to the fortress. Stroszek is still firing single shots from one of the loopholes. After a while they cease.

324. From the houses. The road lies deserted in the morning heat. On the harbor side the abandoned boats. The camera pans slowly to the dead donkey, still lying stretched out in the middle of the road.

325. The dead donkey, close up. Swarms of flies around its mouth, nose, and eyes.

326. Same as 250. From the mast of a ship hangs a desiccated octopus.

Kos, Street

327. Slow traveling shot from the harbor drive to one of the broad side streets that lead from there to the center of town. Women are sitting on their doorsteps looking inquisitively into the camera. A child is leaning against the wall of a house. The camera travels past a hairdresser's shop. The hairdresser is standing in his doorway; he has no customers. Pan to the other side of the street where armed soldiers are patrolling.

Kos, the Harbor

328. View of the fortress. Nothing is stirring. Suddenly a thin pole pokes a few meters over the wall from the inner courtyard with a flag fastened to it. It isn't possible to make out the emblem on the flag because there is no breeze to make it billow. Stroszek can be heard screaming.

STROSZEK'S VOICE: I declare war on all of you if you don't place
    yourselves under my command . . .

Kos, the Marketplace

329. Traveling shot. The camera reaches the large, almost perfectly square marketplace, which is surrounded by houses. Groups of people are gathered. No sounds except Stroszek's voice.

STROSZEK'S VOICE: I am the supreme commander of all the armed forces . . .

330. The small mosque on the left side of the marketplace. In the shade of the tree next to the mosque sit several old men.

STROSZEK'S VOICE: . . . and I'm going to screw you all . . .

331. Close-up. The old Turkish fountain where worshippers used to wash their feet before entering the mosque has waterspouts all around it, but only one is still working. Old inscriptions.

STROSZEK'S VOICE: . . . come out, you cowards, and present yourselves for inspection . . .

332. From a *kafenion*. Tables and chairs extend far onto the square, but hardly anyone is using them.

STROSZEK'S VOICE: . . . then we'll launch a campaign such as none of you have ever experienced . . .

333. In the middle of the square clusters of people are standing and talking. Almost all men. No vivacity in the conversations, subdued gestures.

STROSZEK'S VOICE: . . . show yourselves. I'm going to count to ten: one, two, three, four . . .

334. Market stalls, most of them offering fruit for sale, besieged by wasps. Very little activity. Several stalls situated side by side are deserted because the vendors are sitting together on empty crates, talking.

STROSZEK'S VOICE: . . . I'll show you. I'm going to set your houses on fire tonight, till I burn you out . . . (he laughs)

335. View across the marketplace from the second floor of one of the houses. The crowd is frozen in expectation. Very little movement.

STROSZEK'S VOICE: . . . if anyone attacks headquarters, I'll blow you all to kingdom come.

336. Same as 102. The damaged ancient marble statue. Stern posture, weathered face, blank eyes.

The New Headquarters

337. The large room, furnished only with a long table and chairs. All the maps are still on the table, along with two glasses of lemonade. Nora and the colonel are standing in the room. She appears very collected.

COLONEL: I assure you, we're going to do all that's humanly possible to capture him.

NORA: Will have to shoot at him, you think?

COLONEL: No, we won't shoot at him. That would be too dangerous, because then he could ignite the munitions. The best thing for us would be if he set off more fireworks. That's what he promised to do, so I've been told.

NORA: He still have a lot of . . . what do you call them?

COLONEL: Rockets, fireworks.

NORA: Yes, rockets, I'm sure he still has many.

COLONEL: If he does set off more fireworks, we can overpower him. We've ascertained that he fires them from the inner courtyard and also from the walkway along the ramparts. From there he can't get to the munitions depot so quickly. Besides, he'll be so focused that my people can get over the wall in several places at once, with darkness on our side.

NORA: If you catch him, must he go to a court?

COLONEL: He's ill. We'll send him home so he can be cured quickly.

Nora nods bravely.

338. Same as 117. The wall of the fortress into which an ancient statue has been incorporated, with only the soles of the feet showing.

Harbor

339. The sentry at the lighthouse gives a signal.

340. From the harbor drive. From one of the side streets a truck sets out, dragging behind it a rope with a noose. The truck steers for the dead donkey, makes a half-turn around it, and stops. A man who was running alongside picks up the noose and tightens it around one of the donkey's hind legs. The truck starts up and drags the donkey away.

341. Close-up. The abandoned basket of fish by the gangplank.

342. From the houses two men dart across to the basket and grab it by the handles. They carry it at a run to safety.

343. Same as 250. From the mast of a ship hangs a desiccated octopus.

Inside the New Headquarters

344. In the large room six men are lined up for inspection. One of them is Becker. The colonel marches back and forth right in front of them. The lieutenant is standing at the table, bent over a map.

COLONEL: So, you know . . .

345. The camera follows him as he paces and thus also travels past the faces of the soldiers.

COLONEL: . . . how delicate this operation is that you're about to carry out. Shortly before 1800 hours, when you receive a signal from the sentries, you will move into your staging positions. But you won't go into action until the moment the first rocket goes up . . . . The most important thing is that the wall be scaled in all three places simultaneously. You'll be given the most essential equipment for that: rope ladders, grappling hooks, and in each team the second man will have tear gas. The first man in each team, that's you, and you, and you . . . (he points to three of the soldiers) . . . has to hold his position as soon as he's mounted the wall. The locations have been chosen so you'll be able to see the munitions depot from there. If Stroszek should head for the depot, and this is my strict order, you must shoot immediately and without calling out a warning. Is that clear?

THE THREE SOLDIERS: Yes, Sir.

COLONEL: The second man in each team, that's you, and you, and you . . . (he points out the other three soldiers, among them Becker) . . . must try to get as close to Stroszek as possible. Once you have him surrounded, deploy the tear gas. But if he notices anything before that and makes any sort of move, you must fire immediately.

346. Medium long shot. The colonel puts the men together in pairs.

COLONEL: You two are coming from the northeast corner, you from the gateway . . . wait, Becker, you have to be there; you know the layout best—it's a bit confusing in there. And you two are attacking from the direction of the lighthouse. For you it's going to be hardest to get into your staging position. When you have a chance, you have to run along as close to the wall of the fortress as you can till you reach the only tree, and then take cover there while you wait for it to turn dark.

347. Same as 117. The wall of the fortress into which an ancient statue has been incorporated, with only the soles of the feet visible.

Kos, the Harbor

348. Traveling shot. Becker and another soldier approach the fortress through a park dotted with bushes. Both are armed with submachine guns, and Becker has tear gas canisters dangling from his belt. They have little difficulty reaching the fortress un-

detected, for in the place where the narrow bridge over the street leads up to the gate there are trees with large canopies that block the view from above.

349. Two young soldiers run crouching onto the section of break-water on the far side of the fortress and come to a halt by the sentry behind the cart. They too are armed with submachine guns and tear gas, but one of the soldiers is also carrying a rolled-up rope ladder and a large iron hook.

350. The two soldiers and the sentry from close up. The soldiers have sat down on the ground behind the cart and are panting as quietly as possible.

351. The third pair is waiting with all its equipment in the door-way of a house along the harbor drive.

352. The sentry at the lighthouse gives a signal.

353. Long shot. The two soldiers set off running, first taking cover by the fishing boats drawn up on land.

354. Medium long shot. The soldiers wait by the rusted boats. The soldier carrying the thick bundle with the rope ladder hands his submachine gun to his partner because it's hampering his running.

355. Long shot. The two set off running again, one of them with a submachine gun in each hand. They reach the wall of the fortress and make long dashes until they reach a single tree and a couple of bushes.

356. Long shot. View of the entire harbor and the fortress in the background. No visible movement except Stroszek's flag waving in the rising evening breeze.

357. In a Jeep parked at the corner of a side street stands the colonel, watching the fortress through his binoculars. He is chewing on his lower lip.

358. The rough trunk of an olive tree. The heat has made the bark brittle and fissured. Slight pan downward toward the field in which the tree stands. Parched earth littered with rocks.

359. Same as 141. The empty, transparent exoskeleton of a cicada on the bark of the olive tree.

Kos, the Harbor, Night

360. Long shot. Clear, starry night above the harbor. Lights in the houses. The fortress lies in darkness, without any movement (the camera lingers).

361. In the brightly lit doorway of a *kafenion*, people are waiting, their profiles dark against the background.

362. Close-up. A streetlight surrounded by a dancing cloud of mosquitoes, among them clumsy moths.

363. Long shot. View of the fortress, its outlines dim in the darkness (the camera lingers). Suddenly a rocket shoots up, then a second one. The fireworks display begins as it did the previous day, in an irregular rhythm. Only after a while does it develop into a real spectacle in all its splendor. The rockets shoot into the sky in quick succession, soundlessly, reach their zenith and split into glowing shells (the camera lingers). Suddenly the fireworks show collapses, like a fountain that has been turned off. The fortress lies in total darkness again. No sound can be heard. Long uncertainty. Then a distant shout rings out from the fortress into the stillness.

VOICE: We've got him.

Kos, Open Landscape

364. Traveling shot along a dusty road from the back of a moving vehicle. The landscape disappears from the rear. Rapid movement. Typical karst, littered with rocks. Only isolated olive trees in arid soil that have survived despite the heat and the inhospitable growing conditions. A small caravan of donkeys, heavily laden, toiling along the road. Soon they are out of sight. Cicadas chirping in the heat.

Even Dwarfs Started Small

CHARACTERS

THE PRECEPTOR

PEPE, *inmate, his prisoner*

AZÚCAR, *inmate*

CHICKLETS, *inmate, Azúcar's brother*

ANSELMO, *inmate*

CHAPARRO, *inmate*

COCHINO, *inmate*

GUADALAJERO, *inmate*

HOMBRE, *inmate*

LORENZO, *inmate*

RAÚL, *inmate*

ROBERTO, *inmate*

TERRITORY, *inmate*

MARCELLA, *cook*

AN AUTOMOBILE DRIVER

A POLICE OFFICER

Prefatory Remarks

The title should be understood as simply a working title. It has no bearing on the film. It is important that the word *dwarfs* not be spoken in the film.

The film should be shot in black and white, no matter what.

Numbering of scenes and shots and more specific directions for the camera have been omitted on purpose. The camera will be patient and inconspicuous.

The place described in the script is located in the province of Chiapas in southern Mexico; but conceivably another setting could be chosen, as the particular landscape does not play a primary role.

The essential feature of the film has to do with physical objects and the environment they create, i.e., with the objects' proportions in relation to the people portrayed in this film. A door handle will be a perfectly normal handle, a motorcycle a motorcycle, and a chair a chair, nothing more. Yet by the end of the film the objects will appear monstrous, malevolent, and distorted, while by that time the human characters may be familiar to us, as if they represent normality. Here we have the provocation inherent in the film: that which is appalling may become familiar to us and the familiar appalling.

At the very beginning the film's titles appear in a simple font and in simple graphic arrangement against a black background. Then, likewise against a black background, the following text appears:

> About forty kilometers northeast of the Mexican town of San Cristóbal, for the past eight years youthful offenders have been undergoing preparation to be reintegrated into society by working on a remote agricultural estate. The estate is an "open" institution. Two years ago, while most of the inmates and their instructors were off taking in a festival in a nearby town, a revolt broke out among those who had been left behind for disciplinary reasons.

Yard and General Surroundings of the Buildings, Daytime

Here the images begin. We see it immediately: the revolt has erupted near the barn. Very briefly, in passing, we glimpse a cluster of people scuffling, perhaps ten against two, just for a second; we see pushing and shoving, not real fighting, just an agitated skirmish. Someone peels out of the group and runs off. Right after that a second image registers: these are dwarfs, it is dwarfs who are pushing and shoving. Grotesque figures, Lilliputian bodies, overly large heads, stubby legs, prematurely aged faces. The fact that they must all be adults is something we also recognize in tandem with our horrified realization that these are dwarfs.

All this happens in a second as the camera pans over the scene while following a motorcycle, a roaring motorcycle. We see almost none of the outbreak of the revolt, only what we pick up while flying by over the course of several long minutes, and yet this much becomes clear: the decisive turn of events may already be occurring. With merciless persistence the camera follows the movements of the motorcycle, which is swerving wildly around the buildings and through a building, its motor roaring at deafening volume as it kicks up sand.

The motorcycle is white, an uncanny machine, at least 21.5 horsepower, with gleaming chrome and a whole battery of headlights. A heavy motorcycle, such as killer gangs ride in the United States or ruthless police squads. A low-pitched rumbling, sand swirling behind the rear tire. The handlebars curve high into the air like the horns of a steer.

We notice at once that the rider is also a tiny dwarf, and that he is having trouble controlling it. His stubby legs are too short to hug the tank properly, his hands holding the handlebars are above his head; he is wearing goggles. And now we also realize that this insane ride will not end because the dwarf cannot reach the brakes, that he has no way to stop, that he has to ride until the motorcycle runs out of gas. And over here, as we speed by, we catch sight of a dwarf who is pulling up a fence post. And then, in the dust, the melee for a moment.

Now, pursuing the motorcycle, we see the landscape, the surroundings, the buildings as the dwarf rides and rides.

We recognize that all this must be taking place at a high altitude, certainly more than two thousand meters above sea level, on a flat, almost circular high plateau that stretches for about ten kilometers and is ringed by mountains. No villages. During this entire time intensely white wisps of mist form fringes over the mountains all around. It is a very cold, strange mist along the perimeter, accompanied by a constant wind that never lets up.

Wild plumes of dust are thrown up by the motorcycle, and on the bleak plain dust swirls in its wake. Behind the barn the motorcycle scatters a flock of chickens that have taken cover there from the wind, their feathers ruffled. Led by the rooster and buffeted by the wind, they flee behind the nearest corner of a building but are blown off course, like swimmers swept away by a rushing river.

The plateau is incomparably bleak; a dusty road, coming from a notch in the mountains, crosses it and meanders out of sight into the mist on the other side. Telegraph poles stand along the road, crooked, gaunt, mournful-looking masts carrying hardly any wires. Only one species of tall, desiccated cactus grows here, along with a few thorny, leafless shrubs. Then a dusty cow pasture and a wretched cornfield, where the dead stalks stand far apart. Dust covering everything, now and then a dried-up irrigation ditch plowed into the ground. Blindingly bright light over the landscape.

By the road, not far from the buildings, a small weir made of crumbling concrete. Hard to imagine that there would be any water for it to hold back. Around the almost dried-up body of water, deep fissures in the rock-hard parched soil. Someone can be seen running from the complex and striking out along the dusty road. It is Marcella, the cook. She runs in an appallingly irregular way. The reason it looks appalling is that her legs are so short and her head sits so low over her shoulders. The dwarf on the motorcycle is controlling his machine only with great difficulty and now pursues the fleeing dwarf for a few meters, circling her twice out in the open. Several times he shouts something that we cannot make out, but she does not respond; instead, turning off to one side, she scoots, almost without having to stoop, under a fence and into the cactus fields. Silently, in her hobbling run, she disappears from view.

The motorcycle bucks and leaps, churning up sand and stones. It reaches the buildings again, which stand far apart in a kind of a horseshoe formation. The dwarf struggles to stay on, pressing his legs against the bulging gas tank, and regains control of the roaring vehicle. First we see the administration building and promptly realize that the combatants have just herded each other in that direction. We see shoving around the entrance, and some ornamental plants in tin containers are knocked over. Now real fighting is taking place at the door.

At first glance the administration building seems out of pro-

portion. The ground floor is surrounded by a somewhat pretentious row of arcades with whitewashed columns that support a
broad balcony with a whitewashed balustrade, but the building
has only one story above the ground floor, topped by a flat roof of
corrugated tin.

On the right, seen from the administration building, is the
large barn, a long building, also low, with several large doors
into the yard, some of which are open. The building also houses
a workshop, with machinery standing around, drums containing petroleum, a tractor parked in an open bay. To one side, behind the barn, we see as we fly by long rows of low-to-the-ground
awnings: the chicken coops.

Across from the administration building stands the dormitory, a fairly large structure that was apparently constructed in
haste and promptly left to deteriorate. On the ground floor to the
right, the large kitchen windows; to the left of the building several
tall stacks of lumber in no particular order, and, almost hidden
by them, a small lean-to built onto the dormitory, with a canopy
in front.

As the motorcycle passes this structure, two dwarfs jump up,
waving their canes wildly in the direction of the motorcycle. They
are Azúcar and Chicklets; from their groping movements and
the way they stretch their heads forward to listen we realize that
they are blind. We immediately notice their berets, which they
wear pulled down to their ears on both sides. From the trash,
tools, and assorted dishes strewn around, we can conclude that
these two are housed here, separate from the others.

The buildings have no rational relation to each other; the gaps
between them are too great to allow them to form a meaning-
ful complex. The three unconnected structures merely frame
an empty space, much too wide, across which dusty wind blows
ceaselessly.

On the side where the horseshoe formation opens lies the
road, and beyond it begin fenced-in dismal pastures with a few
open animal sheds, and behind the buildings are a bare tree and
a dreary soccer field with only one usable goal; the other one has
already been taken over by cacti.

Plumes of dust continue to rise as the dwarf rides and rides. Passing the entrance to the administration building we see for a second that the melee by the door has now intensified and that one of the dwarfs is trying to drag another into the building while all the others are trying to prevent it. For the space of a moment it becomes clear that the blows being exchanged are somewhat hesitant, and now we also catch sight of a billy club in someone's hand. The cacophony of voices drowns out the motorcycle.

A VOICE: . . . my foot in the door! . . . my foot's caught in the door!

One dwarf splits from the group and runs toward the motorcycle, which is now zooming around the wide courtyard. It is Hombre. Coming closer, we can now see the face of the dwarf on the motorcycle; it is Cochino.

HOMBRE: Stop!

COCHINO: I can't!

HOMBRE: Jump off; he's dragging Pepe into the house! Hurry!

COCHINO: It must be almost out of gas. All we put in was two cupfuls.

The motorcycle bucks and keeps circling the bleak space between the buildings as sand swirls behind it. The machine continues to roar for almost another minute, then the motor suddenly sputters loudly and dies. Out of inertia the motorcycle briefly keeps going in a smaller loop toward the road, slows almost to a crawl, then tips to one side as it comes to a stop. The dwarf Cochino jumps off, executing an involuntary somersault, and lands under the fountain of sand that the rear wheel kicks up with its final revolution.

Now we can get a good look at Cochino's leathery, wrinkled face and his overly large, powerful hands. He struggles to his feet, pulls off the goggles, which are coated with dirt, and sets out in an appalling dash to join the other dwarfs around the entrance to the administration building.

The fighting there has died down, the melee is over; the door is now closed. Several inmates are still pushing against the door, which looks enormous. We are among the dwarfs.

Some of them are storming the door, slamming their shoulders into it; their shoulders do not even reach the handle. Territory, still fairly young and apparently the strongest one, stands out. Taking a theatrical running start, his shoulders hunched forward, he hurls himself at the door, even though the effort is clearly futile.

Off to one side sits the dwarf Anselmo. He has lost his right shoe and is rubbing a contusion on his foot. He cautiously peels off the lacerated skin and pops it in his mouth. Tiny Guadalajero comes over to him.

ANSELMO: My shoe's inside. My right shoe's in there. My foot got jammed in the door.

GUADALAJERO: Let me peel, too.

ANSELMO: Only if you let me see what you have in there.

Guadalajero does not answer. Instead, he clings more tightly to a cigar box he always carries around, clutched under his right arm. As a result, Guadalajero's movements are impeded.

The Area across the Road

Several dwarfs by the fence that encloses the cow pasture. They are pulling skinny fence posts out of the parched ground and wrapping thick tangles of barbed wire around the upper end to make ferocious-looking clubs. One of them, Lorenzo, strikes his club on the hard ground several times to test it. To make it look very menacing, he swings the club high above his head before bringing it down. The dwarfs work in feverish haste, with two of them grabbing each fence post and rocking it until it comes out of the ground. Cochino has joined in. He is in a particular hurry because he missed the beginning. Frantic haste. Cochino and Lorenzo tackle a post together.

COCHINO: Why did Roberto let himself get caught in the act?

LORENZO: He didn't let himself get caught; it was the others.

COCHINO: Why the others?

RAÚL: (mockingly): Why the others? Why the others? We wanted to have our turn.

LORENZO: The others realized what was going on out in the barn, and they wanted to have their turn (he rocks the pole fiercely). Pull this way, come on, don't be a wimp . . . . At first Marcella went along with it, but then it got to be too much for her, there were too many at once.

RAÚL: She's not used to that.

LORENZO: Right, and then she screamed for help.

RAÚL: And now the teacher has Pepe in the house with him, and Pepe, the poor dummy, wasn't even involved. We're going to get him out. That stinker has to let him out. (He digs the dust with his club.)

Outside the Administration Building

By now Territory is the only one still attacking the locked front door. Anselmo wants to try a closed window shutter, but he cannot quite reach it. So with his left foot, on which he still has a shoe, he kicks a tin container, with a plant still in it, over to the window and climbs onto it.

ANSELMO: My right shoe is in there.

He suddenly rattles the shutter in a rage, pounding it with his fists.

ANSELMO: Open up—my shoe's in there!

TERRITORY (pauses briefly to collect his thoughts): Territory.

On one side of the administration building Roberto and Chaparro, a particularly small dwarf with huge hands and feet, have begun tossing their clubs at the telephone line that enters the building there. Like hammer-throwers they twirl their clubs, which are longer than they are tall, over their heads and hurl them into the air. The barbed wire on Chaparro's club has begun to come loose on one end and gets hung up on the line, where it remains dangling. Roberto throws his club at it several times but cannot bring it down. He also hits the telephone line, but his club ricochets to him. Every time it is hit, the line groans, and then it suddenly breaks right at the wall and comes whipping down. Anselmo appears around the corner, running with only the big toe of his right foot hitting the ground.

ANSELMO: My shoe's inside and he has all the windows closed.

CHAPARRO: Watch out, don't step here.

ROBERTO: It's certainly live.

He picks up his club and pokes at the line lying on the ground. Then he carefully coils it up and leaves it hanging from the nearest telegraph pole.

Yard in Front of the Administration Building

Now all the inmates have clubs, with which they pound on the door, getting in each other's way as they do so. Guadalajero has seized a pitchfork with his free hand, while from the barn Territory drags a jack meant for a truck, so heavy that he can hardly move.

HOMBRE: We want Pepe!

RAÚL: Let him out, we want Pepe!

Chaparro and Roberto come around the corner, with Anselmo trailing behind them.

ROBERTO: We got the line down. I got the line down.

CHAPARRO: Now we're getting Pepe out.

LORENZO: Pepe, can you hear us?

HOMBRE: Pepe, we're going to break the door down.

Hombre strikes the ground and then the door handle to re-
inforce his promise. The actions being carried out by the door
seem half-hearted, but in each other's presence the dwarfs want
to appear determined and bold. Still, they get caught up in
their performances. All those involved get caught up in their
performances.

ANSELMO: My shoe must be right inside the door and to the right.
(He takes a step back and listens to his own words echoing.)
Hey, Pepe! We're breaking down the door now!

ROBERTO: We want Pepe!

THE INMATES (howling in unison): We want Pepe! We want Pepe!

They begin to beat on the door, but less, it seems, in order to
break it down than to make noise and challenge the preceptor.
But no reaction comes from the target of their siege. Guadalajero
strikes one of the tin planters with the tines of a fork, making it
hum. Territory uses his jack to smash an orange crate, while all
the rest watch. The racket increases.

Seen from the yard. Suddenly the preceptor up on the second
floor steps to the balustrade of the balcony. His age is hard to
determine; he must be somewhere between thirty and fifty, more
likely fifty. His face is rosy but covered in hundreds of tissue-like
wrinkles, as when one crumples up tinfoil and then smooths it out
again. His neck and the lower part of his face are mottled from
all the agitation. He is so small that he can barely see over the
balustrade. His head rises and falls a little because he apparently
has to stand on tiptoe to be seen and stretches to his full height
only when he shouts really loudly.

PRECEPTOR: Stop it! Have you all lost your minds?!

Wild bawling is the only response from below. The dwarfs
move a short distance from under the arcades into the open area
so as to have a better view of the preceptor. They assume threatening poses.

PRECEPTOR: I haven't done anything to you! What have I done to you?

ROBERTO: We want Pepe!

THE INMATES (in unison): We want Pepe!

LORENZO (shouting down the rest): Pepe, we're coming!

PRECEPTOR: Lorenzo, be reasonable. You're the most reasonable one here . . . . Quiet! Quiet down!

But the inmates shout all the more loudly, a wild cacophony.

PRECEPTOR: Chaparro, Territory, Hombre, be reasonable!

HOMBRE: Come down here if you want something of us. It's easy to talk when you're up there.

RAÚL: Come out here, and we'll give you what you have coming.

PRECEPTOR: I'm calling the police if you don't quiet down this minute!

ROBERTO: Calling the police; he wants to call the police. (Defiant howls.) Just go ahead and try.

RAÚL: We're going to bash the door in now.

THE INMATES (all shouting at once): We're bashing the door in! Pepe, we're coming to get you!

PRECEPTOR: Stop! You must have lost your minds!

Screaming and shouting, the dwarfs hurl themselves at the door, this time more determined to show that they mean to break it down.

PRECEPTOR: Stop it; be quiet this minute! Quiet!

ROBERTO: Come out here first, let Pepe out.

PRECEPTOR: I'm calling the police right now; you know what that means!

COCHINO: The line's been cut for a while already. Go ahead and try.

RAÚL: Police, hah! They have their techniques, but we figured them out a long time ago.

They pound on the door and the window shutters. A dull roar. The preceptor, at his wit's end, his voice cracking:

PRECEPTOR: Quiet! If you don't quiet down immediately, you'll be sorry!

Suddenly the inmates pause, realizing that the situation is turning serious. Territory goes ahead and smashes a bench with the jack, but hesitantly. Brief silence.

GUADALAJERO: He's going to do something to him. He'll kill him.

ROBERTO: He wouldn't dare.

Still somewhat hesitant, the inmates back off a little farther into the yard. The preceptor has disappeared from the balcony, and the door to the room in which he has barricaded himself is closed.

ROBERTO (trying to provoke him): Go ahead and try! Do something to him!

LORENZO: We want some excitement. We've had it with this joint.

Although somewhat irritated by the silence coming from the administration building, the inmates do not trust themselves to defy the preceptor as directly as in the beginning. The farther they move from the building, the less threatening they appear. As they withdraw toward the barn, making all the more racket, they reveal that they intend to pitch their revolt at a somewhat lower level for now. Thus threat and counterthreat reach a kind of equilibrium.

Room inside the Administration Building, Interior

First we see Pepe, who is tied down rather sloppily in a wicker chair but is so obedient and long-suffering that he does not dare to move. He sits very quietly and passively, staring at the file cases on shelves across from him and then raising his eyes to the ceiling. The rope with which the preceptor bound him to the chair was apparently too short, for Pepe's left foot is tied to the left leg of the chair with an extension cord that still has its plug and socket on the ends. Pepe's short legs hardly reach halfway from the chair seat to the floor, and his back rises no higher than a pillow one might place to cushion the backrest. Pepe's age is hard to guess, but he seems to be younger than the preceptor. A first glance at Pepe's face suggests that he is feebleminded; his mouth is usually half-open, and some spit is always dribbling out.

The room is rather sparsely furnished and has the dreariness typical of Mexican provincial government offices. A desk, a few chairs, a coat rack, a good-sized shelving unit for files, and some potted plants make up the entire decor. Scrubbed floors, a French door onto the balcony, and a window, both closed. On the wall behind the desk a small painting of a saint with an illuminated flashlight bulb that serves as an eternal light, next to it a photo from a police sports tournament.

The photo from close up: standing on two motorcycles traveling side by side, about ten policemen have formed a pyramid. The man on top has both arms stretched out like wings, an insane image because all the participants are dwarfs. In the foreground a dwarf police officer with several stripes on the sleeve of his uniform. His revolver, hanging at his side from an ornamental white cord, extends from his hip to his knee.

Pan from Pepe around the room. At the desk the preceptor has made a show of picking up the telephone and dialing a number, so his prisoner can clearly see what he is doing.

PRECEPTOR: I'm calling the police now. They can be here in half an hour with a helicopter. They won't take their Jeeps.

He listens into the receiver and lets his prisoner think he has reached the police.

PRECEPTOR: Hello . . . yes, this is the station, this is the detention center . . . . Listen: send backup forthwith, preferably by helicopter, yes . . . a first unit, right, make it snappy. A rebellion has broken out here . . . . I'm surrounded. Make it snappy, before they smash everything to bits . . . make it snappy . . . yes, yes, I'm all right for now . . .

The preceptor hangs up and comes toward Pepe from behind the desk.

PRECEPTOR: I'm going to push you to the window now, and you'll tell them that the police will be here soon.

He starts pushing the squeaky wicker chair to the window; the preceptor's head hardly reaches above the chair. Pepe struggles to find words but is completely helpless because he plainly can hardly speak. He strains and strains and is extremely embarrassed. The preceptor pauses.

PEPE: Can't do it.

PRECEPTOR: Have you forgotten what I just said—again?

Pepe nods in embarrassment; he is so ashamed that he appears even tinier in his chair.

PRECEPTOR: (soothingly): Come on, you can do it. You've been so good about learning things already. You remember this sentence, I'm sure: "We want to live a good life, because why else would our mothers have endured such pain to bear us?"

PEPE (happy because he does remember the sentence): Yes! Yes, yes!

PRECEPTOR: All right, pay attention now: you tell them that the police are coming, that the police will be here very soon . . . . Have your forgotten again?

Pepe nods weakly and does not dare to move.

Yard by the Barn

All the dwarfs have gathered in front of the barn, most of them still holding their clubs. Territory is fiddling with the jack's mechanism. The dwarfs have a straw beehive in their midst and are trying to prove to each other how brave they are by blocking the entrance with a wad of newspaper. They bat at the agitated bees that are buzzing around them. Raúl has set fire to a piece of cloth soaked in oil, which gives off dense smoke. He's using it to try to drive the bees away from the entrance to the hive. Roberto finally manages to plug it.

HOMBRE: Hey, Roberto, don't make it so tight. It has to be very loose, because otherwise it won't open again.

GUADALAJERO: There must be honey in there, from so many little bees.

LORENZO: Quick, Cochino, get some string from the kitchen.

Room in the Administration Building

The preceptor is trotting angrily back and forth in the room. His tone toward Pepe has changed noticeably.

PRECEPTOR: We're in a pretty pickle now . . . . Why did you have to let yourself be caught, you idiot? Right? Damn it, I don't know how anyone can be such a fool. You really could have been more careful, couldn't you? I'm telling you, we won't have another idiot like you here. Why would you run without noticing that the others weren't behind you, without even looking? What choice do I have?

Pepe becomes even more embarrassed and helpless; he's terribly ashamed of having caused so much trouble.

PRECEPTOR: I can't let you go now, you have to understand. What would the others outside think? Right? It would be the same as my hanging a white flag out the window and saying, "Gentlemen, here I am, at your mercy. Please come in and smash the place to pieces so at least you've finished the job . . ." As long as I keep my composure, it's still possible to get things under control. By the time the director gets back, order must be restored. The director will have to see that I've proved myself in a situation like this . . . . I mustn't show fear, because otherwise they'll become completely unmanageable, won't they? At least Marcella's safe from that mob . . .

From the courtyard, at some distance, the dwarfs can be heard shouting, sounding considerably more self-assured than before.

Open Area in Front of the Administration Building

The dwarfs cross the yard in a pack. In the middle Roberto is carrying the straw beehive, which now hangs on a string like a birdcage. They are hooting and hollering, crowding together. They stop in front of the arcades and spread apart somewhat to make way for Roberto, who now swings the hive over his head.

RAÚL: Come out, or we'll smoke you out! (Howls.)

LORENZO: Come out, you lazy son of a bitch; we want to duke it out!

CHAPARRO: We want Pepe!

THE INMATES (in unison): Pepe! Pe-pe!

RAÚL: We're going to fumigate the place now!

From the yard. Suddenly the preceptor comes out onto the balcony and strains to look over the balustrade. He has collected himself, and it is clear that he has regained his air of authority, which immediately provokes the inmates.

PRECEPTOR: The police will be here soon; they can be here any minute.

Wild shouting and laughter greets his statement.

ROBERTO: How's that? You don't believe it yourself!

CHAPARRO: The line's been cut for ages already.

ANSELMO: I hope they really do come. We want to go into town again, to the whorehouse. A person could die here.

(Shouts of approval.)

ROBERTO: We want a chance to get our hands on some floozies for a change. We're sick of going jogging to suppress our animal instincts. We want to go to the whorehouse. Now we're going to smash this whole joint to smithereens.

PRECEPTOR: We understand; after all, we were young once. But now you need to be decent again.

ROBERTO: Decent—that's a joke. Come down here, and we'll show you what decent looks like . . . . When we do something good, no one gives a hoot, but if we do something bad, no one ever forgets.

PRECEPTOR: I'm getting the police here immediately . . .

The preceptor's words are almost drowned out by the cheering for Roberto. At that moment Roberto swings the beehive over his head and hurls it at the building. But instead of flying onto the balcony it smashes against the balustrade, breaks apart, and falls back down. A swarm of bees escapes, and the dwarfs scatter, but they promptly regroup. The moment the hive became airborne the preceptor disappeared behind the balustrade. Now he pops up again.

PRECEPTOR: That's enough! If you don't quiet down this minute, something's going to happen to Pepe. You're going to the dormitory now!

GUADALAJERO: Do something to him, go ahead! That's exactly what we're waiting for.

COCHINO: Yes, do something to him—you wouldn't dare.

LORENZO: We're going to smash everything to bits, and still you don't dare.

COCHINO: Pepe, kick him in the butt and make him do something to you.

Taunting, triumphant shouting because they all realize that the preceptor is merely making threats and they have the upper hand.

ANSELMO: We're going to hang the cat!

THE INMATES (in unison): Yes, hang the cat!

ANSELMO: We're going to break the chickens' necks!

GUADALAJERO: We're going to behead the chickens!

ANSELMO: We're going to sic Azúcar and Chicklets on each other!

THE INMATES (in unison): Right! Right!

ROBERTO: We want to see what kind of trouble we can stir up in this joint.

COCHINO: Pepe, kick him in the butt. The cowardly son of a bitch doesn't dare lift a finger.

Yard in Front of the Barn

Full of excited haste the dwarfs are trying to take the largest of the barn doors off its hinges. The bolt is mounted so high up that they need a pole to open it. The door swings open. The dwarfs force the grips of their clubs under the huge door, which the wind keeps swinging shut, and use the clubs as levers.

Close-up. The door can be seen coming off its hinges. Now the door is hanging crooked in its frame. The dwarfs dart back a few paces, leaving their implements behind, to avoid being hit by the door when it falls. A gust of wind catches the door and smashes it against the barn wall. From there it tips, remaining suspended for a while, then gradually falling out of its frame. Finally it crashes to the ground, raising a cloud of dust. The dwarfs promptly close in on the door, joining forces to lift it and let it fall again. But because they can raise it only a little, it makes hardly any noise this time. So they abandon this activity and look around for something more rewarding. Their eyes light on the various supplies stored in the barn. They rip open sacks and cardboard boxes.

Finally, Territory comes upon a stack of commercial-size tins of powdered milk; dropping the car jack, he storms into the open with one of the tins and proceeds to dump the contents as a wind gust passes through. For a second, Territory is surrounded by a fog of the flour-like powder, which then blows across the courtyard in a long plume. Territory is ecstatic.

TERRITORY: This is my territory!

Roberto dumps out two tins at once.

ROBERTO: We're done drinking this stuff. What do they think we are, calves?

RAÚL: It's been coming out of our ears for far too long.

HOMBRE: Hey, Territory, let's fog him in and then launch our attack.

COCHINO: No, first we're going to tear down the fences, and then we'll drive an ax into his head.

Lorenzo calmly empties a tin in front of the barn, creating a cloud of powder.

GUADALAJERO: That won't get him to come out, I'm sure; he won't come out for something like that.

ROBERTO: We've got to find Marcella; then we can grope under her skirt till she squeals; that'll make him come out.

COCHINO: We're not going to find her; she ran into the cacti over there, and now she's over the hills and far away.

ROBERTO: Then let's let all the cows out so we don't have to deal with lousy livestock anymore . . .

GUADALAJERO: But he won't see any of that . . .

ROBERTO: . . . the lousy "interaction with animals and fields and pastures that brings out the best in people."

GUADALAJERO: . . . he won't see it, or at most, if he comes out on the balcony.

ROBERTO: You can be sure he'll notice when they're gone.

In the Pasture

At some distance. The dwarfs break down a fence, felling a thick post with two axes whose handles, when they stand them on the ground to catch their breath, come up to their shoulders. Much shouting to attract attention, to let the besieged preceptor know that something is happening out in the pasture. At this distance it is impossible to make out the individual dwarfs, except for Territory, who is carrying the jack. At some distance from the others he drags it to a telegraph pole, where a dwarf is already busy with a saw. Territory leans his mighty tool against the pole at an angle to widen the cut.

Anselmo can be recognized because he is picking his way among the cacti with one shoeless foot and is so focused on watching for thorns that he cannot be of any help.

The telegraph pole falls slowly, creaking and pulling the two skimpy lines with it and raising a spinning cloud of dust. The other dwarfs come to look.

Closer. The dwarfs crowding around the sawed-off pole. Chaparro keeps the others away from the cable on the ground. Territory, full of pride, swings the jack onto his shoulder with a nonchalant expression, though he sways slightly under the weight.

CHAPARRO: Watch out, there's bound to be current in there.

LORENZO: Why? The line's already broken at the house.

CHAPARRO: You still have to be careful. The current may come from the other direction.

ANSELMO: I have a thorn in my foot. I stepped on a thorn and it went into my foot.

RAÚL (pointing to the downed line): Why don't you step on that, then?

(Laughter.)

HOMBRE: What's the point of cutting down the poles? It does no good if he can't see it.

LORENZO: First of all, it was sawed down, and second, whatever's down is down.

HOMBRE: Right, but it's just a utility pole. Let's break down the fence now and let the bulls in with the cows . . .

(Loud cheers.)

... don't we want to see the immediate effect out here in the wild ...

(Raucous cries)

... in beautiful nature? And after that we'll cut down the vultures' sleeping tree!

COCHINO: Right, the tree where the vultures sleep!

HOMBRE: The one he's so proud of because it's the only tree for thirty kilometers around.

COCHINO: Let's roast a vulture and tell him ...

HOMBRE: Rubbish, we're cutting the tree down.

ANSELMO: I'm not coming; there are too many thorns. It's not safe to walk.

At the Vultures' Tree

Close-up. Packed in tightly, drowsy vultures are perched on the tree, their necks retracted between their shoulders, their heads bent. Now and then, to get more room, they peck at the birds next to them with their sharp beaks. Mostly they sit motionless on the bare branches.

The tree looks bleak because only a small portion of it still has leaves. Most of the trunk and limbs are almost devoid of bark, weathered smooth and bleached almost white. A blow with an ax makes the whole tree shake. The vultures lift off ponderously, while some remain on the branches.

We can see the entire tree now, down to its roots. At the base, where it widens, the dwarfs have surrounded what appears to be the gigantic trunk and are hacking away at it with axes. The tree stands near a barbed wire fence, beyond which the cacti begin. The last few vultures flap off languidly and reluctantly but land in a half-circle quite close by, where the other vultures are already waiting.

The dwarfs set to work eagerly, although they must have realized at once that they will be thwarted by the rock-hard trunk. Finally, after making no headway with axes, they try the saw, but it is much too small for the trunk, which they have to attack down at the bottom where it merges with the roots. Farther up, it would be quite a bit easier, but they cannot reach that high.

They try sawing the tree from several sides and push wedges into the cuts, but the saw gets stuck. Territory attempts in vain to force his car jack into one of the cuts, but the ground is too sandy and the device bores its foot into the sand. After a while the dwarfs abandon the saw, after proving to each other that there is no point continuing. One last time they brace themselves in a half-circle against the trunk. A crazy spectacle: eight dwarfs trying to push over a tree at the roots.

ROBERTO: Let's set it on fire; this isn't going to work.

Guadalajero is pushing diffidently with only his left hand because he still refuses to put down his cigar box.

GUADALAJERO: Let's spread Weed Begone around it; then it'll die.

LORENZO: Are trees weeds?

HOMBRE: Besides, that would take at least half a year to work—that's crap.

The vultures in a half-circle in the sandy pasture, almost motionless. One vulture gives a couple of lazy flaps with its wings in the direction of the tree. Another follows it listlessly, seemingly not caring, while the others huddle there half-asleep.

In the Pasture

A fence dividing the pasture into two sections has been leveled; strong wind and dust, white wisps of mist on the mountains in the distance. The dwarfs, who do not even come up to the cows' rumps, drive several of the cows from one pasture into the one where the bulls are sitting chewing their cud. It is not easy to get the cows to budge; they too are sitting in groups chewing their cud. Chaparro has ripped a fleshy branch off a cactus and uses it to prod a recalcitrant cow to her feet.

The meeting takes place without any sparks flying; both parties pay no attention to each other, not so much as reacting to each other's smell. Cochino throws a stone at a cow to keep her from sitting down again.

COCHINO: Come on, get up! Don't you cows have any feelings? Don't you ever go into heat?

Chaparro, the tiniest of the dwarfs, takes on a mooing bull that obviously wants to be left alone to chew his cud. With a running start like a sprinter, Chaparro leaps into the air and kicks the bull in the hindquarters. The bull bucks a few times reluctantly and, when Chaparro tries to drive him toward the cows, trots away looking cross.

The other dwarfs, unwilling to be shown up, bravely follow his example. One of the cows, which Raúl has badgered to her feet, kicks with both hind legs and knocks Raúl over.

RAÚL: Damn you!

LORENZO: Come on! Let's see you mount each other!

COCHINO: We're going to light a fire under them!

Infuriated, the dwarfs pursue the cows, which are now galloping away, and throw stones at them because they cannot keep up with them. The herd stampedes, mooing, as dust flies.

Raúl struggles to his feet and shakes the sand out of his clothes. The others approach him.

RAÚL: Damn these stupid cows!

GUADALAJERO: Did she hurt you? Let me see.

RAÚL: No, I'm fine. Just got sand up my nose.

Raúl spits, then blows his nose with two fingers. Anselmo comes, stepping cautiously with his unshod foot, his face full of self-pity. The dwarfs stand around indecisively for a while.

ANSELMO: What a mess.

COCHINO: Apparently they never go into heat.

ANSELMO: What are we doing way out here? Besides, there are thorns
   everywhere . . . . Come on, let's go back to the house and do
   something that'll make him come out for real.

In the Yard

Wide view. The inmates obviously have a plan. They have gathered
around the fallen barn door and are putting their heads together,
whispering. Roberto gestures emphatically. Nothing stirring in
the administration building. The besieged preceptor is keeping
perfectly still and not showing his face.

   The group of dwarfs from closer up. They have made their plan
and are all clearly in agreement as to what they're going to do
next. They whisper, speak in low voices, although there is no one
far and wide to hear them.

ROBERTO: This won't work unless there's plenty of noise.

LORENZO: Right, we'll smash all the windows.

ROBERTO: There aren't enough of them.

LORENZO: Then we'll just take all the plates and cups.

COCHINO: Will that really make enough noise?

TERRITORY: Territory!

COCHINO: The plates won't be loud enough.

   A broad pan over the entire yard, lying there deserted. Only
wind and dust, nothing else stirring. We know something is about
to happen. The door and windows of the administration building
are still closed up tight. Only a few chickens, almost featherless,
their remaining feathers fluffed, struggle through the wind to a
protected corner of the yard.

In the Barn, the Open Garage Area

The dwarfs have moved to the part of the garage where the tractor
and several agricultural implements are parked in an open bay.

Hitched behind the tractor is a heavy harrow. One can tell by looking at the tractor that it has been used on hard, rocky ground. On the side where some motor oil has dripped on the hood, a lot of dust has stuck. The tread on the large rear tires is almost worn off.

Roberto tries to mount the tractor, but the iron steps are too high for him. He stacks up several orange crates and laboriously scrambles onto the tractor. Once on top, he gets into the driver's seat, which he does by facing the seat and raising one knee, pulling himself up onto the seat and only then turning around, like a small child getting onto a chair. Perching on the very edge of the contoured seat, he can just barely reach the far too large steering wheel, which he turns this way and that to see if he can move it.

In front, near the engine, Cochino and Anselmo have helped Territory onto one of the small front tires and are supporting him from below so he can reach the open hood from the side. Territory struggles to his feet and sticks his head into the engine compartment, almost disappearing in the process. Only his legs and his posterior are visible.

TERRITORY: Wrench.

No one hands him one; the dwarfs watch him but at first do not understand.

TERRITORY: Wrench!

Lorenzo is the first to catch on and hands a wrench up to Territory. Territory fiddles with the engine for a while. The others gaze almost reverently.

Territory stretches his hand behind him, opening and closing it.

TERRITORY: Wire!

Wire is passed from hand to hand, quickly, as the dwarfs try to be helpful. Lorenzo hands it up to him.

COCHINO: It stinks that the key isn't in it.

HOMBRE (indicating Territory with his head): He know what he's doing; he's already stolen sixty cars.

Territory has attached the wire to the engine somewhere and now he pulls his torso and head out of the compartment. He half-turns to the others.

TERRITORY: Territory!

Territory then reaches into the engine one more time with the wrench and closes a circuit. The engine comes to life with a rumble, chugs a little unevenly, but then catches. Territory jumps off. Roaring loudly and emitting billows of smoke from the upright exhaust pipe, the tractor stands in its bay, shuddering to the rhythm of its motor.

The Yard outside the Barn

The inmates hurry out of the barn. When all of them are outside, Roberto tries to shift the tractor into gear, but he cannot reach the clutch. So he slides forward out of the driver's seat and shifts into first gear from a standing position. Because he has to lean back slightly to reach the steering wheel above his head, in this unnatural position he releases the clutch too quickly, and the tractor goes shooting wildly out of the barn, dragging behind it the rattling harrow, which kicks large quantities of sand into the wind.

View from the administration building. The tractor is not moving very fast. Roberto struggles to control it and drives around in a circle for a while. Some of the dwarfs run alongside. Still standing, Roberto manages to get into second gear; the tractor is now moving faster, but still at a moderate speed. Roberto steers in circles a few times in the middle of the yard, then he lets the steering wheel lock in position and jumps off to one side to get out of the way. He picks himself up off the ground.

ROBERTO: There, that'll give us the noise we need. Not bad, I say.

The tractor keeps circling by itself, keeping to a tight orbit, on and on.

Yard in Front of the Administration Building

The dwarfs have taken up positions under the balcony and are yelling. They drown out the noise of the tractor behind them. The tractor is circling all by itself.

THE INMATES (in unison): Pepe, Pepe!

RAÚL: Let Pepe out! Come out! Something's about to happen!

COCHINO: Come out, you cowardly son of a bitch, let Pepe out!

RAÚL: We're going to do something any minute now.

No answer from the house; nothing stirs. The preceptor is keeping perfectly still in his room. The house seems deserted.

By the Dormitory

The dwarfs sneak on tiptoe along the outer wall of the building, heading for the stacks of boards; Anselmo hangs back because he is afraid to walk on his bare foot. Even farther back is Guadalajero, who is clutching his cigar box and clearly does not want to expose it to any danger.

As they proceed, it becomes apparent to us that they are planning to do something to Azúcar and Chicklets. The closer they get to the stacks of boards, the more cautiously they scout out the situation up ahead. Behind them the tractor continues making its lonely, roaring rounds. Roberto directs the others: when they reach the boards, on a hand signal from him they spread out quietly.

Among the Stacks of Lumber

The camera picks out the small lean-to built onto the dormitory that is half-hidden by the stacks of lumber. The entrance is shaded by a small canopy supported on two posts. From one post a sturdy rope stretches to a water pipe attached to the side of the dormitory. Around the lean-to lies a ring of discarded food cans and other garbage, but the area immediately in front of the structure has been painstakingly swept clean.

Beneath the canopy, which is roofed with tar paper, two orange crates face each other, padded for sitting on, one with articles of clothing, the other with an old blanket, folded. Between them is a somewhat larger crate that serves as a table. On it are two plates, some bread, and a kettle. From the open entrance to the lean-to, an electrical cable extends to the side of the table, powering a small electric hot plate with a single burner. The white enamel on the three-legged base of the hot plate has almost completely flaked off.

Here we see Azúcar and Chicklets going about their usual activities. Azúcar, who is wearing his beret pulled down almost to his eyebrows, shows remarkable dexterity as he tends the hot plate, on which something is cooking in a battered pot. We see dried blood above the root of Azúcar's nose.

The dwarf Chicklets, somewhat smaller than Azúcar, likewise wearing a beret, which he has drawn down over his ears, is groping his way along the rope to the spigot, where he fills a metal canister to the brim. These two are the only inmates wearing short pants, much too big for them, from which their bony knees protrude. They make a thoroughly derelict impression.

No matter what they are doing, the two hang on to their knobby canes, greasy and shiny with wear, even though the canes often get in the way. Their body language expresses constant wariness and suspicion, including toward one another. From the similarity of their features we can tell they must be brothers.

Carrying his water, Chicklets carefully feels his way back to the cooking station and places the container on the ground next to Azúcar. He gropes for his brother's hand and guides it toward the handle. Azúcar picks up the container and pours some water into the vigorously steaming pot, while almost at the same time shooing Chicklets away with a fierce swish of his cane. Chicklets backs off, two steps out of Azúcar's range, and squats on the ground.

Azúcar raptly seasons the steaming food in the pot. The roar of the tractor's engine continues unbroken, the volume increasing whenever the tractor comes closer to the lean-to on its rounds.

From the lean-to. Through a gap between two stacks of boards we briefly see the tractor passing, dragging the harrow. Then we see the faces of Hombre and Cochino, as they cautiously peer out of their hiding places. The dwarfs are sneaking up on the brothers. Lorenzo darts by on tiptoe, hunched over. From farther to the right Anselmo approaches on hands and knees, carefully moves an empty tin can out of his way, and crawls closer. The dwarfs use any available cover, although that would not really be necessary, since Azúcar and Chicklets are blind.

Roberto is the only one who has recognized the obvious; now he emerges, upright and completely visible, taking two strides from behind a stack of boards on the left. He then holds still until the tractor passes nearby again and at that moment takes another cautious step forward.

View of the lean-to. Azúcar now turns away from the pot, still steaming slightly, and sets up nearby a row of tin food cans of various sizes. In the middle of the row he places an empty bottle.

Chicklets uses a rough bundle of twigs to sweep all larger pebbles away from a stretch that extends five or six meters from where Azúcar is standing, then taps his way with his cane past Azúcar, who almost reflexively lashes out at him with his cane as he goes by, and into the lean-to. From there he brings a wooden ball, several more food cans, and a bottle.

View from Azúcar and Chicklets. We see that they are now surrounded by the other dwarfs, who are closing in on them very cautiously. But they are still largely out of reach, except for Roberto, who has moved even closer, completely visible. Guadalajero wants to get a rather large sheet of tin out of his way, using only his left hand. Roberto turns toward him with his finger on his lips; Guadalajero leaves the tin where it is.

View of the lean-to. Several meters apart, Azúcar and Chicklets have each set up a row of cans like a battle line, and each line has an empty bottle in the middle. They signal the position of their cans to each other. Azúcar begins, starting with the can at the very end, tapping his way along the line, striking each can, and now we realize that the cans are arranged in such a way as to make higher and higher sounds toward the middle.

Chicklets is the first to deploy the wooden ball. He waits until Azúcar has tapped lightly two more times against the bottle in the middle, which sounds the highest note, and then, with great concentration, he rolls the ball toward it. But his aim is not very good, and the ball hits the can at the very end of the line.

Chicklets is dissatisfied with himself and now taps on his bottle in the middle. In the meantime Azúcar has managed to locate the ball, which had bounced off to one side, and he takes his turn trying to hit Chicklets' bottle. He has aimed well and promptly hits a high-sounding can right next to the bottle.

Then Azúcar taps his entire row and strikes his bottle two more times. At the very moment when Chicklets sends the ball rolling, the tractor roars by. Chicklets' aim was very accurate this time; the ball rolls between the bottle and the can next to it in such a way that it hits both. Chicklets feels so happy that he pounds the ground with his cane. Azúcar is annoyed and uses his cane to makes a grating sound on the ground, obviously negative. Then, to signal where he thinks the ball struck, he taps on the can to the right of the bottle. Chicklets disagrees and furiously taps his bottle to indicate that his ball hit the middle.

Sitting about five meters apart they begin to quarrel wordlessly, using knocks as signals. Finally, Chicklets throws his bottle at Azúcar, barely missing him; the bottle smashes against the wall of the dormitory. Azúcar lashes out wildly with his cane and swings it above his head, making it hiss a warning. Then they calm down a bit, listening warily.

From the lean-to. The other dwarfs have crept closer and wait until behind them the tractor roars past again with the rattling harrow. Roberto, leading the pack, takes a few more large steps and then holds still. He is the first to have reached the open area in front of the lean-to.

In the meantime Azúcar and Chicklets have abandoned their game and returned to their meal preparations. Azúcar is stirring the pot while Chicklets comes tapping out of the dark entry to their living place, bringing utensils. Azúcar turns off the hot plate and gives the pot a final stir.

Chicklets takes one of the two plates and holds it out to Azúcar, knocking to get his attention. At the signal, Azúcar holds out his hand for the plate. With a ladle he carefully fills the plate, a task he accomplishes with remarkable skill. Then Chicklets holds out the second plate to him, and both of them feel around to make sure that the plates contain the same amount of food. The first plate receives a bit more to equalize the portions. The brothers sit down opposite each other on their orange crates to eat. Chicklets slices bread for both of them, which they also check suspiciously to make sure the quantities are exactly the same. As the noise from the tractor swells again, Roberto suddenly appears in the frame. He is now only a few steps from the table.

The other dwarfs, having likewise closed in, remain motionless, some of them hidden behind the stacks of lumber. They do not come any nearer because Roberto has already managed to get so close. He holds his breath.

Azúcar gets up and feels his way into the lean-to, barely missing Roberto, who stands there like a pillar of salt. Roberto then seizes the opportunity to advance three paces, using a gust of wind and the roar of the tractor as cover. Very slowly and carefully he removes Azúcar's plate from the table, stopping dead in his tracks when Chicklets interrupts his meal to listen. Chicklets then goes back to eating while Roberto stands there holding his breath, the plate trembling in his hand.

The dwarfs all around hold their positions, hardly daring to breathe. It seems like a long time before the tractor comes by again.

With utmost concentration Roberto next takes two very cautious steps to one side, then stands motionless as Azúcar comes out of the lean-to and passes very close to him again, bringing tin cups and a coffeepot. Azúcar places the coffeepot on the edge of the table, and as he passes his hand over the surface he immediately notices that his plate is missing. He puts the cups on the ground and reaches for Chicklets, his hand landing in the middle of his brother's plate.

With a furious gesture Chicklets grabs his plate. Azúcar finds the table empty and now tries to snatch the plate from Chicklets. An appalling, murderous fight ensues; the two dwarfs strike out at each other with their knobby canes, knocking over the improvised table. Their sticks hum menacingly as they brandish them over their heads.

Roberto is still standing like a statue very close to the action, the full plate in his hand. As he pursues Azúcar, Chicklets bumps into him. Roberto drops the plate, thereby revealing his presence to Azúcar. The dwarfs by the lumber piles break out in jeers. In a flash, Azúcar and Chicklets take in the situation and, flailing wildly with their canes, grope helplessly in all directions.

View of the lean-to. Now the dwarfs leap out of their positions among the boards, hooting mercilessly. They dash by the blind dwarfs and then duck out of the way of the wild flailing. They tap the brothers on the shoulders and scream their names.

RAÚL: Chicklets!

LORENZO: Chicklets! Chicklets! Chewing Gum, Chewing Gum!

RAÚL: Hey, Chewing Gum!

CHAPARRO: Sugar! Hey, Sugar!

ROBERTO: Azúcar!

GUADALAJERO: Azúcar, over here!

Azúcar and Chicklets strike out madly in all directions, a scene terrible to behold.

As the blind brothers, their faces distorted with rage and frustration, flail in all directions, the other dwarfs try to get them closer to each other, at which they finally succeed. In the process Lorenzo receives a dreadful blow on his back and takes off running without a sound. Then a blow smashes Anselmo's right hand. He bellows in pain but does not run. Chicklets strikes out like a madman, his face now ecstatic. Suddenly, as he slices the air, he catches Azúcar on the ear. The blow knocks Azúcar to the ground, where he utters a brief, uncanny cry. The other dwarfs stop egging them on.

GUADALAJERO: We've got to separate them.

COCHINO: No, let them be so we can see which one is stronger.

Chicklets goes after Guadalajero, who takes to his heels. The others run after him, chortling triumphantly. Visible through a gap between the stacks of boards, the tractor continues to circle.

Room in the Administration Building

At the door to the balcony the preceptor has climbed onto a chair and is observing the goings-on in the yard through a gap in the curtains. Pepe is sitting meekly in his wicker chair, intently focused on the ceiling. From outside the tractor can be heard roaring. Apparently the inmates have gathered under the balcony again; they are shouting up to the preceptor.

ROBERTO'S VOICE: Come out! Chicklets is killing Azúcar!

HOMBRE'S VOICE: Come out, the two of them are killing each other!

ROBERTO'S VOICE: They're going to beat each other to death with their canes! Someone's got to intervene. They wanted to kill us, too!

HOMBRE'S VOICE: We're going to hang Chicklets!

GUADALAJERO'S VOICE: Or we'll ram an ax into Chicklets' head!

ROBERTO'S VOICE: And then we'll scalp you! (Wild cries and braying laughter.)

The besieged preceptor does not stir. The jeering inmates depart but remain in the vicinity of the administration building. The group is breaking up, as one can tell because individuals can be heard calling out to each other.

The preceptor scrambles down from his chair, facing the backrest and lowering one leg until he can touch the floor, while he kneels with the other leg on the seat. In this way he somewhat laboriously reaches the ground. He moves aimlessly around the room, speaking partly to Pepe.

PRECEPTOR: Something must have happened to Azúcar . . . but I'm
not going out there, that would just make everything worse,
wouldn't it? Better to accept a lesser evil than to lose the whole
show. They're bound to beat each other to death someday in any
case, those two . . .

RAÚL'S VOICE (alone): Pepe, why aren't you doing anything? Give
him a kick in the butt to make him come out. It's time for us
to take him on!

PRECEPTOR: . . . If we separate them, they won't eat till they're
almost starved. And if we put them together, they'll kill each
other. Right? There's nothing we can do.

Pepe, who obviously has not followed, nods obediently.

PRECEPTOR: We can't put them in with the others; that turned out
very badly right at the beginning. Maybe it was wrong, but it
can't be changed now. Or what would you do if your parents put
out your eyes so they could send you out to beg? You'd be like
that, too.

PEPE: Yes, yes, yes.

ANSELMO'S VOICE: A dressing for my hand.

The Yard

From the administration building. The tractor can be seen making its ghostly rounds. The orbit has shifted, the circles becoming
somewhat lopsided. Now the tractor comes closer to the administration building and also closer to the barn, shifting its path
almost imperceptibly away from the dormitory and the road.

The dwarfs have broken into several groups. They have qui-
eted down somewhat and seem indecisive. Roberto, Chaparro,
and Territory are sitting near the barn with Guadalajero, pes-
tering him to open his cigar box. Guadalajero enjoys being pes-
tered; he clutches the box all the more firmly. Raúl is over by the
administration building, using one of the clubs lying around to
pound on the door and the wall, then taking what remains of the

bench Territory smashed and hurling it in front of the tractor as it passes. The tractor rumbles over it, crushing it with a crashing, cracking noise. A corner of the bench gets caught under the harrow and from now on is dragged around the yard, making an ugly scraping sound.

In the background, near the stacks of boards, Cochino and Chaparro are chasing a large sow across the yard, followed by a posse of squealing piglets. Chicklets and Azúcar, who picked himself up again, are swinging their sticks over their heads as a warning and bringing them down hard on some boards. Chickens go running in all directions.

Room in the Administration Building

The preceptor, seeking support and affirmation, addresses Pepe, who sits there apathetically, showing no resistance as the words rain down on him. He squirms in his chair a bit but does not dare to strain in earnest against his loose bonds.

PRECEPTOR: . . . I mean, we do make mistakes sometimes, but our intentions are always good, aren't they? . . . The day Chaparro arrived, we had him join the soccer game, remember? And afterwards, in the washroom, don't you remember?

Pepe struggles to remember, but nothing comes to him. He is very embarrassed and terribly ashamed.

PRECEPTOR: Don't you remember the business with the jacket? Chaparro didn't take his off, but that way you can't really wash your hands properly, right? I tell him, "Take off your jacket, you can't wash your hands properly. We take our jackets off here . . . ." But he didn't do it, just acted as if he hadn't heard. So I think to myself, just wait, buddy, I'm not putting up with this . . . . There was no way I could've known. So I say to him, "Look here, Chaparro, that's not good enough, it's just a lick and a promise." I had to say that, right? Well, he doesn't say a word, just stands there and won't take off his jacket. So I say to him—

and there was really no way I could've known—"Come on, take off your jacket, the jacket has to come off now, no joke." Well, he starts to cry and takes off his jacket, without a word. He was so embarrassed in front of the others. The sleeves of his shirt were in shreds and black with dirt and actually moldy. No one ever took care of him, certainly not his mother . . . she'd run off with a custodian . . . . But that same day I, together with the director, handed him a new shirt in the presence of all the others, and that made me so happy. This profession, our profession, does have its good sides . . .

In the Yard, by the Barn

Lorenzo comes running to the group huddled around Guadalajero, jumping out of the way of the tractor. Even at a distance he waves agitatedly.

LORENZO: The sow . . . (he pants hard); they've killed the sow, Chaparro and Cochino have.

ROBERTO: What? Which sow?

Behind the Dormitory

All the inmates crowd at a respectful distance around the huge sow as she lies there, her body almost completely covered with bristles, stretched out motionless on the ground. The inmates are half taken aback that now something has actually happened that was not just intended as a provocation. The sow's hind legs are stretched out in terrible rigidity almost in a straight line with her body, while her front legs are crossed over a hole they gouged in the sand. She has a ghastly distorted expression around her mouth, her upper lip dreadfully drawn up toward her snout. Six piglets are still suckling at the dead sow's teats.

GUADALAJERO (irritably): Why did you have to go and kill her?

CHAPARRO: We're not telling; it's none of your business.

ROBERTO: How did you do it?

COCHINO: We're not telling . . .

ROBERTO: Come on, tell us how you did it! Then we can finish him off, too!

CHAPARRO: Shut up, it's none of your business. You never had to herd the pigs.

COCHINO: That's where my name comes from: *cochino*, piglet.

Chaparro tries to dispel the atmosphere of irritable embarrassment, as if things had not just taken a serious turn, as if the only intention had been to provoke the preceptor.

CHAPARRO: We're going to drag the beast to his door now—that'll make him come out.

ANSELMO (relishing the situation): Yes, let's do that. I can't wait to see his jaw drop. But I won't be able to help you pull—my hand's messed up. Don't we have any bandages?

The inmates try to make light of the situation, as if it represented the best chance of luring the besieged preceptor out of his hiding place.

In the Yard

View of the stacks of boards. From behind the dormitory, on the left, almost by the road, the inmates are struggling to drag the enormous sow past the boards and into the preceptor's field of vision. They have grabbed the legs and are moving the animal in infinitesimal jerks. Roberto is pulling the sow by the ear. Nearby the piglets dash about in dire confusion.

The inmates do not get far because suddenly Azúcar and Chicklets burst out from behind the boards with terrible, silent determination and fall upon them. They take to their heels, half-relieved to escape from a situation that they cannot quite admit to having brought on themselves. The sow is left lying there. Azúcar and Chicklets, who have routed their enemies, feel their way around the dead pig in amazement.

View across the Yard

Now it looks as if things have settled down of their own accord. The yard is deserted; only the tractor still makes the scene outrageous. As it continues its ghostly circling, the broken piece of bench under the rattling harrow scrapes horribly over the sand and stones. In the course of its increasingly lopsided circling it has come ever closer to the corner of the barn nearest to the administration building. It is also passing closer to the arcades, where it runs over a club lying nearby.

Now the sky above the pastures is filled with vultures, circling calmly and silently. In the distance blindingly white, cold mist veiling the mountains.

The inmates are squatting quietly and somewhat indecisively in a close circle around Guadalajero, near the barn door they pulled off its hinges. But as the tractor comes by too close for comfort, they retreat halfway inside the storage area. They begin egging each other on with brazen talk, trying to hide their indecisiveness and embarrassment by expressing increased interest in the contents of Guadalajero's cigar box.

Guadalajero enjoys finding himself the center of attention and takes his time. Close-up. All the others appear very impatient, but apparently they already know what is in the box.

HOMBRE: Come on, now, let's see what the little ones are up to.

RAÚL: Do you have new ones?

GUADALAJERO: Yes, two. Two new ones.

Guadalajero solemnly opens the box. Tight close-up. We immediately take in a velvet lining onto which various insects are neatly pinned. And we promptly discover the bizarre feature of this collection: all these insects are wearing tiny articles of clothing tailored just for them and are arranged to make up a wedding procession. With the reverence of someone who has spent weeks painstakingly working in this miniature format to provide the procession with clothing, Guadalajero removes the insects one at a time and introduces them.

GUADALAJERO: I've finished the bridegroom. See, this grasshopper. The little tuxedo looks good on him, doesn't it? Fits him to a T. I used high-quality jacket lining. And the shirtfront looks adorable.

He holds up the bridegroom, a grasshopper in black tails and a white shirtfront, turning the pin carefully between thumb and forefinger to display him from all sides.

ROBERTO: Ho ho, that's what we'll do to him, too. We'll get him out here and drive a spear through him, and then we'll tailor a tuxedo for him just like this one.

HOMBRE: Nice! We'll pin him onto a velvet cushion. Ha ha.

(Hesitant jeers resume; the dwarfs are getting into the spirit again.)

ROBERTO: Come on, let's go measure him for his tux.

But no one stirs. The inmates wait as Guadalajero carefully returns the grasshopper to its place and now takes out the bride, a dragonfly with a delicate veil on her head and a tiny white lace dress on her body. Her exquisite transparent wings have been left free.

Anselmo shows little interest.

ANSELMO: We've seen her, we've seen the bride already.

GUADALAJERO: Yes, but the veil is all new . . . such a fine little creature.

He pins the dragonfly back in place on the velvet lining. After her, as the first members of the procession, he points out a few tiny mosquitoes, but they do not have clothes yet.

GUADALAJERO: Hmm, unfortunately . . . the problem with the maids of honor hasn't been solved yet. With little mosquitoes like this, see, it's hardly safe to handle them . . .

Instead he takes out a bumblebee and a disgustingly hairy tarantula.

GUADALAJERO: With these, it's much easier . . . . But still, the sweater for the spider took me three weeks. He has eight little arms, after all.

COCHINO: What do you mean? Spiders have only six legs.

GUADALAJERO (deeply offended): Go ahead and count them. Here: one, two . . . three, four, and these here, and see, seven, eight.

COCHINO: Well, I guess this kind has eight. All insects have six legs. I know that for a fact.

RAÚL: Yes, if we pull off two, this spider will have only six.

HOMBRE: We'll pull off the teacher's legs. That'll get his attention.

ANSELMO: We'll rip his butt open to his collar.

(Wild cries of enthusiasm.)

GUADALAJERO: This little bumblebee is still missing some items. Up to now all it has is a necktie, a tiny silvery-gray necktie.

The next creature is a beetle, dressed in a shirt and trousers. Perched on its head is a tiny top hat.

GUADALAJERO: The bridegroom's supposed to get a hat just like this one, like the best man's. The hat isn't hollow inside, that I admit.

CHAPARRO: Guadalajero, do you know how beetles get into Heaven?

GUADALAJERO: No, why?

CHAPARRO: Well, that's something a person's got to know. So, you pick the beetle up, and then you feel terribly sorry for him because he's so alone. (He raises his voice in a mock expression of sympathy.) Poor little beetle, you have no father, you have no mother, no brothers, no sisters, you have no one in the whole wide world.

Chaparro makes a hollow in his hand and speaks to an imaginary beetle.

CHAPARRO: . . . no one at all. Would you like to see the good Lord, would you like to go to heaven? Yes, and then, then you do this . . .

With his right thumb Chaparro crushes the imaginary beetle in his hollow left hand to a pulp, twisting his thumb several times. Guadalajero is indignant, his feelings hurt; the others bray with laughter.

CHAPARRO: Let's ask the teacher . . . ha ha ha . . . whether he wants . . . ha ha . . . to see heaven.

(Wild laughter.)

ROBERTO (bent double with laughter): Stop! I can't laugh anymore!

LORENZO: No, I know what we should do: let's get him and stick his head in quicklime . . .

GUADALAJERO: Oh, come on!

LORENZO: My cousin did that once to someone in a bar. There was this fat son of a bitch, and he was completely plastered, with a neck as fat as a pig. And all of a sudden the son of a bitch pulls out a gun and shoots my cousin's little dog. You should have seen him. He grabbed him by the porky neck . . . two more shots hit the door jam, you can still see the holes . . . and he took him and pushed him headfirst into the quicklime . . .

GUADALAJERO: We don't have a limeworks here. But look at this, this little fly and her cute little coat. Fits her perfectly, and check out the high collar!

ROBERTO: Oh, leave us alone with your jabber. We have to get Pepe out. What are we doing sitting around here? If he doesn't let Pepe out immediately, we're going to make all hell break loose.

COCHINO: Come, we'll set fire to the place. Then we'll see if he comes out.

ROBERTO: Right, let's see the joint go up in flames. This place is killing us. I need to get to town.

ANSELMO: At least there are floozies there.

In the Yard

Wide-angle shot of the terrain. Everything still makes a peaceful impression, with the exception of the tractor, which is still circling, coming ever closer to the corner of the barn. Long, lingering shot, as if this is the calm before the storm. Wind, some chickens, the grating sound of the wood under the harrow. The tractor roars uninterruptedly, with the steering wheel locked in position and exhaust puffing out of the upright pipe. In the background Azúcar and Chicklets with the dead sow.

A closer shot of the sow. In the meantime the animal's stomach has swelled in the heat and is distended. The hind legs are still appallingly straightened; the ghastly expression around the snout remains unchanged. Azúcar and Chicklets are working over the sow with their feet, kicking her stomach. That releases the bloat with a lifeless fart; two of the piglets flee in distress.

Now Azúcar scrambles gleefully onto the dead sow and rides her in a gallop to compress the bloated body. Flies have already landed in black swarms around the animal's eyes, mouth, and nose. In the background the tractor circles past.

The inmates have scattered over the yard and seem determined to storm the administration building. They have picked up various long poles and other implements. Raúl is pounding on the locked door again, shouting something.

From the barn. The inmates are busy with preparations. In the background, past the road lie the cow pastures, with a few vultures in the air. Suddenly, a complete surprise: an old, rather battered car pulls off the road, an older-model Chevrolet with pretentious fenders and the scarred quality characteristic of everything that passes through this countryside. Some of the dwarfs take to their heels. At this moment Anselmo, who is now going around completely shoeless and has a bandage on his injured hand, is by the road. Cochino is with him, holding a club. Both of them are so surprised that they stop dead in their tracks.

The car screeches to a halt in a cloud of dust. A man can be seen inside. The door opens, but no one comes out. First, a small stepladder is lowered from the door, then a dwarf dismounts from his raised seat. He immediately notices Azúcar and Chicklets, who are riding the sow nearby, and the tractor, still making its driverless rounds, but apparently he finds all this perfectly natural. He makes a point of not showing any surprise at these odd phenomena. Led by Roberto, the other inmates now approach him.

THE MAN: Excuse me, is this the road to Dolores Hidalgo?

ANSELMO: Yes, stay on this road, and it's over there beyond the mountains.

COCHINO (pointing with his club in the opposite direction): Going by way of San Cristóbal would have been shorter—there aren't so many mountains.

In the background one hears a faint cry from the administration building, where the besieged preceptor is trying to catch the stranger's attention. The man probably hears the voice in the background over the noise of the tractor, but, with an expression like that of a postman unwilling to get involved in a private marital crisis overheard through an open door, he scrambles up his stepladder into the car and pulls the ladder in after him. He rolls down the window on his side and politely ignores the increasingly desperate cries from the administration building.

THE MAN: Thank you. Thank you very much.

ANSELMO: Just stay on this road. You can't miss it.

The car drives off, rattling, in an enormous cloud of dust, toward the distant mountains.

Room in the Administration Building

Very agitated, the preceptor struggles to regain his composure. He makes the impression of a castaway who has just seen the last ship that could rescue him pass by without noticing him. Pepe plainly feels pity for him; it strikes him, too, as terrible that the car has driven on.

PRECEPTOR: When will another car come by, when does a car ever
   come by? . . . At most once every two weeks. He didn't hear
   me . . . . Or maybe he did hear me and is going for reinforcements . . . . Soon they'll have wrecked the tractor, too; it took
   us eight months to get it delivered . . .

The preceptor paces rapidly back and forth, straightening the
objects on the desk. Suddenly, he turns on Pepe, cowering in his
chair.

PRECEPTOR: And what am I supposed to do with you now?

Pepe doesn't answer, can't find the words, but would clearly
like to say something. He simply can't get out a single word. The
preceptor calms down a little and speaks to him in a slightly more
friendly tone.

PRECEPTOR: What should I do now? Do you have any idea? If I
   keep calm, I can probably hold out until help arrives, don't you
   think? If they don't do anything worse, I won't lose face . . . .
   well, they've been quiet for a while now . . . . The director, maybe
   the director will get back with the others earlier than expected
   this evening; that's perfectly possible. They can be here before
   nightfall, can't they? What would you say?

Something has occurred to Pepe, but he cannot express it
properly. He tries to say a few words but gets stuck and then stops,
ashamed at not being able to get it out. Pepe goes back to staring
at the ceiling.

The preceptor scrambles onto the chair by the door to the
balcony, using his knee again. Suddenly, Pepe moves, tugging
cautiously at his bonds and trying to get his right hand, which is
tied to the chair, into his pants pocket. He is tied so loosely that
he finally manages, by bending his wrist this way and that, to
reach the pocket. With his hand awkwardly twisted to the back
he gradually pulls out a handkerchief and finally gets a coin between his index and middle fingers. With great effort he bends

forward and pops the coin into his mouth. The veins in his neck bulge with the effort.

In the Yard

In front of the administration building. Lorenzo and Territory are dragging a rug across the yard, dodging the tractor. They reach the other inmates, who are making an exasperating racket as they dismantle a large typewriter in front of the balcony. They show no signs of agitation but on the contrary proceed coolly and methodically, with concentration.

As calm and unperturbed as a dentist, Roberto yanks a typebar out with pliers and then one key after the other. Cochino and Hombre hold the machine steady. Raúl is using a small hammer to scrape a hole in the ground, into which he sticks the already removed platen upright; he then drives it with precise, powerful blows deeper into the ground.

RAÚL: Now we're planting platens.

LORENZO: Come out, you son of a bitch, we want to see some action! Let us have Pepe!

ROBERTO: Pepe, kick him in the butt till he can't take it anymore!

RAÚL (with a final blow he has driven the platen all the way into the ground): Now things are going to pop. We're going to smash everything to smithereens if you don't come out!

TERRITORY: Territory!

CHAPARRO: Why wait any longer? Let's just smoke him out.

Room in the Administration Building

The dwarf Pepe has bitten the coin in two, is holding the halves between his lips, feeling them with his tongue. He spits the pieces onto the floor. The preceptor on his chair turns toward him for a moment but cannot see what has just happened. He peeps outside again.

In the Yard

In front of the administration building. Roberto takes what remains of the typewriter and throws it under the rear wheel of the tractor, which is just passing. The tractor runs over the almost unrecognizably demolished machine and flattens it into the sandy soil.

Now Lorenzo energetically takes a scissors to the rug. Territory begins to tug on the fringes.

LORENZO: Come on, let's make a nice pattern in this rug!

The inmates bellow defiantly and attack the rug from all sides, pulling at it and tussling, with much shouting.

LORENZO: Stop, don't pull so hard yet. First, we're going to cut a pretty pattern into the rug.

HOMBRE: And then the one in there will get a nice pattern in his gullet! . . . We're coming in if you're scared to come out!

Without particular haste and with rapt concentration the dwarfs bite the rug into several large pieces and systematically and with great patience pull the pieces apart until they have a pile of wool.

Territory finally seizes one of the bigger remaining pieces and runs after the tractor with it. He tries to get the piece under the harrow in the rear but does not immediately pull it off. So he waits until the huge tractor has reached him on its next round and throws the large fragment under the harrow, where it actually catches on an iron hook. Territory then jumps onto the piece of carpet, grabs onto the harrow, and, crouching there looking triumphant, lets himself be towed around the yard twice.

THE INMATES (in unison): Territory! Territory!

The cloud of sand and dust behind the harrow gets to be too much for Territory; he jumps off as the tractor passes the other inmates and turns several somersaults. Great applause for this performance.

ANSELMO: Soon the tractor's going to knock these columns down. He'll come out of his own accord when the floor collapses under him. All we need to do is wait and twiddle our thumbs . . .

RAÚL: It's about time the whole shithouse collapsed.

GUADALAJERO: No, look, it's going to hit the corner of the barn first. It almost did this time.

ANSELMO: We don't need this lousy barn and this lousy tractor anymore. We want to go to the whorehouse!

RAÚL: Right, right! We've had our fill of this joint.

In Front of the Dormitory

The action has become more intense; the inmates are going about the business of destruction with great effect, but at a more hectic pace and with increasing displays of rage. Everything seems to be concentrated in the kitchen.

Through one of the large closed kitchen windows a heavy pot comes flying with a rattle of broken glass; plates follow, smashing as they hurtle through closed panes. From inside someone uses a broom to shatter the remaining intact parts of the window. At regular intervals one of the inmates tosses cups through the opening. Metal pots are slammed against the wall; more and more rattling pots join the crazed racket, then a whole stack of plates comes flying through a smashed window frame. Total devastation is being wreaked on the kitchen at top volume; the point is clearly to make sure the goings-on can be heard and understood for what they are.

Yard by the Lumber Piles

Azúcar and Chicklets have jumped off the dead pig. They have begun to bicker and now stand facing each other menacingly, swinging their canes in the air above their heads and bringing them down on the ground with a crash.

Yard by the Barn

Now the tractor has come so close to the barn that on every round it runs over the door that was torn off its hinges. Here the broken piece of bench has been scraped off the harrow. The barn door creaks and cracks under the tractor's huge rear tires and one corner gets bent up in the air. It falls flat with a crash once the tire's weight is no longer on it. Dust swirls up and whirls along the front of the barn. The chickens, huddling in a corner where they have some protection from the wind, do not stir. The racket from the dormitory increases.

Kitchen in the Dormitory, Interior

In the midst of the tumult, we perceive the following almost at the same moment: it already looks as if vandals have struck. Shards of glass all over the floor, tables and chairs upended, several dwarfs hacking away at chairs with the frenzy of berserkers. The dwarfs are trying to reach above the stoves and are having trouble getting pots down from there. We glimpse Territory for a moment in a cloud of flour, smashing a chair he has picked up by one leg against a stove. Guadalajero is holding his cigar box in both hands now to protect it, bent almost double over it while with both feet he stomps on a large metal pot. The dwarfs are screaming and shouting with glee.

Somewhat to the rear of the room Roberto in one sweeping gesture knocks a tall stack of plates off a shelf. Roberto is shouting louder than all the rest.

ROBERTO: No more plates! No more peeling potatoes to improve our character!

COCHINO: We're done eating slops!

TERRITORY: Territory! Territory! Territory!

Somewhat on the edge of the chaos we now see Hombre sitting on the floor with an electric blender that is plugged into the wall. Hombre is filling the glass container usually used for liquids with flour. Leaving the lid off, he turns the machine onto high. With one turn the flour bursts out of the container as if it were the chimney of a locomotive and for a moment fills the entire kitchen with a cloud of white.

Raúl and Anselmo are side by side, banging on the wall and the tiled floor in unison with large frying pans, before focusing entirely on the floor because it makes more noise.

A wild scene for a moment around the table, which is being dragged back and forth through the crunching broken glass on the floor.

ROBERTO: All this junk has to go!

CHAPARRO: Yes, out the window, we want the whole kitchen out in the field!

ANSELMO: My hand! Look out for my hand!

LORENZO: Let's send the kitchen out to Mother Nature!

ROBERTO: We're not eating any more hay! To hell with these disgusting vitamins!

CHAPARRO: No more saying grace!

LORENZO: No more hand washing!

(Wild bawling.)

The inmates begin to pitch any movable objects out of the kitchen window, by now completely destroyed. Pots fly, dishes, two handfuls of forks, half a chair, brooms, canned goods, now the table as well; five inmates hoist the table and send it hurtling out the window, followed by flour, a bucket, the baking sheet, and a wire basket full of spoons. Suddenly silence sets in.

In the background, almost unnoticed, Cochino has tried to knock down a birdcage suspended from a nail above the kitchen door. In the cramped cage sits an ancient parrot, yellowing and already partly bald, which is perched calmly on a rod.

GUADALAJERO: Leave him up there!

ROBERTO: Yes, leave him up there.

COCHINO: All right. We can roast him later. He's been getting on my nerves for a long time. He won't talk and won't talk and has been sitting there for four and a half years, always facing south.

Just as suddenly the tumult resumes. All the scouring powder goes flying out the window, scattering everywhere, and at the same time dish towels and an armful of cups. The craziness ebbs slowly, almost imperceptibly.

LORENZO: And now we're going to water the flowers.

COCHINO: Right, with petroleum.

Yard in Front of the Dormitory

The pile of debris outside the smashed kitchen window is hardly noticeable, with the exception of the table, which landed unbroken, its legs sticking up. The tractor is still circling, coming perilously close to the barn. The barn door, which it keeps running over, is by now completely crushed.

The dead pig lies abandoned by the stacks of boards, and there is no trace of the piglets. Azúcar and Chicklets are also nowhere to be seen.

The inmates come storming out of the dormitory, hauling flowerpots from the building. On the ground floor by the door someone hands the pots out a window, and hands reach up to receive them. As a result of the pushing and shoving around the pots, the plants are already in bad shape by the time they land outside. Through a closed window next to the other one a pot containing a fairly large-foliage plant comes flying almost at the same time as others from a second and third window.

Closer. Cochino lines up the potted plants that are not already in pieces and pours petroleum on them from an oily bucket.

COCHINO: These weeds are going to get a good soaking.

RAÚL: The whole building is full of greenery. But why do we need two hundred pots? Five would be plenty.

LORENZO: We've had enough of pretty flowers that are supposed to make bad children good!

COCHINO: Let's go, set a match to them!

Cochino lights the petroleum-soaked flower stalks and foliage plants himself. They immediately catch fire like torches, sending up black, choking, oily smoke.

From a closed window on the second floor a potted foliage plant comes flying as if eager not to miss out on the action, reaching the ground in shreds. Guadalajero, Anselmo, and Territory come out of the building.

The flower stalks hiss, sizzle, and crackle as pitch-black smoke eddies about in the wind. Wild cries of triumph from the inmates meant for the besieged preceptor.

From behind one of the piles of boards Chicklets suddenly stumbles with a fresh laceration on his forehead that's bleeding heavily. His beret is askew, he's lost his cane, and his knees are shaking.

HOMBRE: Hey, here comes Chicklets.

CHAPARRO: Something's happened to his head.

HOMBRE: Quick, he doesn't have his cane: let's grab him.

They rush at Chicklets and seize hold of him from all sides. Chicklets flails about for a moment, tries to bite, but then lets himself be dragged away without resistance. He is losing a lot of blood; his whole face is smeared with it.

Yard by the Administration Building

The inmates cross the yard in a pack, dragging the badly injured Chicklets in their midst. They come to a halt in front of the balcony of the administration building, take up positions, and thrust Chicklets to the front.

ROBERTO: Come out here! Come out this minute! We've killed Azúcar!

ANSELMO: Now it's Chicklets' turn. And then you're next.

ROBERTO: Look, we've already given Chicklets a new hairdo. Before a person gets strung up, he has to look his best.

COCHINO: Come out here or we'll set this joint on fire. See, it's already burning over there.

Looking up at the balcony. Nothing stirs. Down below one of the inmates in the tight cluster stomps on Chicklets' foot. Chicklets lets out an inarticulate cry and sinks his teeth into Lorenzo's sleeve. Lorenzo struggles to shake him off. Chicklets' head is shaken back and forth.

Up on the balcony the door suddenly flies open and the preceptor steps out, stretches to his full height above the balustrade, sinks for a moment from his tiptoes, and then appears again. He has lost his composure and gazes dementedly in all directions. At the moment of his appearance the inmates break out in infernal bawling.

PRECEPTOR: For God's sake, come to your senses.

With each of his words the inmates' screams grow louder; they can see now that they have shaken the preceptor to his core.

ROBERTO: Shut your trap. We're going to fix things around here the way we want them.

ANSELMO: We've already cleared out the kitchen!

(Bellowing laughter.)

ANSELMO: And Chicklets has a new hairdo. Azúcar gave it to him because no one was keeping an eye out.

PRECEPTOR (firmly): Quiet down now! I want it quiet this minute!

This change in tone sets the inmates off anew. Territory winds up and with all his might hurls a clump of clay at the balcony that hits the wall and breaks apart.

LORENZO: Come out here, we're going to ream your butt, you cowardly son of a bitch.

ROBERTO: Send Pepe out to us so we can set this place on fire.

PRECEPTOR (his voice cracking): If you don't quiet down immediately, something's going to happen to Pepe!

Triumphant bawling from below. The inmates realize that the besieged preceptor is showing more and more weakness.

ROBERTO: Go ahead and do something to him, you yellow dog!

GUADALAJERO: You said that earlier, but you don't have the balls to do anything.

ROBERTO: Come on, Pepe, poke him in the back so he does something to you.

LORENZO: Come on, let's get the chickens ready for roasting. We're going to pluck the chickens. We're going to pluck your tail!

PRECEPTOR: Quiet! I'm going to say as I do.

ROBERTO (screeches): He's going to say as he does!

PRECEPTOR (correcting himself): I'm going to do as I say! I'm really going to do it.

He gets ready to go and do something to Pepe, which the inmates greet with dreadful cries of applause. But at the door the preceptor turns and addresses them again.

PRECEPTOR: Quiet! If you don't quiet down . . .

ROBERTO: Come out here, you filthy son of a bitch!

PRECEPTOR: If you don't quiet down . . .

LORENZO: Shut your trap!

PRECEPTOR: I'm going to do something to him. I need some room. I'm going to do it now!

The preceptor disappears into the room and at breakneck speed brings a chair out onto the balcony.

He disappears again immediately. Amid the jeering laughter of the inmates he hauls file boxes out of the room and stacks them on the balcony. One can hardly see the preceptor anymore behind the balustrade, only the objects he is bringing out onto the balcony. After another stack of files comes a coat stand, which is pushed into a corner of the balcony. It looks as though the preceptor is trying to gain time, as if he is posting warning signs to demonstrate that he is ready to take desperate measures. His movements, to the extent they can be made out from below, are strangely theatrical.

The inmates recognize that this is an act. The besieged preceptor continues to move the contents of the room onto the balcony, acting with oddly intense haste. The number of objects keeps increasing.

Down below at the entryway Territory pounds on the locked door with feet and hands. The inmates throw rocks up at the balcony, but the preceptor pays the missiles no mind. The yelling continues.

Chicklets is pushed under the arcades. No one is paying any attention to him. There he crouches, listening fearfully. His face is covered with blood, but the wound has stopped bleeding. The lonesome tractor rattles by, coming very close.

From the barn we hear screeching and cracking sounds. Now we see that the tractor has run into the corner of the barn and is hung up there. It pushes a post partway over but does not come to a halt. The tires kick up sand and dirt. The tractor grinds away wildly and irregularly, and a board splinters against the radiator. The inmates run triumphantly to the barn. At that moment the steering wheel is dislodged by a jerk of the front wheels and the tractor is partially freed. It ploughs another meter into the building, its front tires and nose smashing into the board wall and suddenly turning in a different direction. It roars through the space between the barn and the administration building, tearing down a wire fence and heading out into the fields, cutting a track through the tall cacti. The harrow drags plants and earth with it.

The inmates chortle, losing all self-control. They follow the tractor for about a hundred meters but then let it go. In a cloud of dust the tractor disappears into the distance. The inmates promptly turn their attention to the chickens, chasing a whole flock from their long, low coops behind the barn. Tiny Chaparro grabs a skinny mule that has been staked out behind the barn. The mule is nibbling on some dethorned fleshy cactus branches it has been given.

Territory pursues the chickens energetically, and once he has caught up with them throws himself on top of them with his whole body. Raúl grabs by the wing a fluttering bird that is shedding feathers and another one by the leg. Now we also see that most of the chickens have disgusting naked necks and featherless rumps. A disease has left them with bald butts. The inmates seize these revolting chickens at random.

Anselmo has stayed back at the corner of the barn; he is completely barefoot and still has his hand bandaged. He pulls a board out of the barn wall that the tractor broke. Guadalajero joins him without having caught a chicken. Behind him comes Chaparro with the mule. In the background the flower stalks are still smoldering by the dormitory.

Yard in Front of the Administration Building

Guadalajero and Anselmo run back to the administration building, followed by Chaparro, dragging the mule behind him by its tether. The other inmates come tearing back with squawking chickens. Feathers fly, dust swirls. Chicklets is still crouching under the arcades, completely apathetic.

Looking up at the balcony. The dwarf up there is struggling to push the large desk through the door. Files are piled high. There is much scraping and creaking. The balcony has been almost completely filled. The preceptor can no longer be seen, only the furniture and everything else he is discarding. Now we recognize the telephone, which he must have ripped out of the wall. Part of a bookcase is now tipped onto the balcony over the desk, which has apparently got wedged in the doorway. The preceptor is working with feverish haste.

Down below Chaparro brings the mule; Territory and Roberto are the first to arrive with their hideous chickens.

CHAPARRO: Now you're going to get what you deserve; we're going to set the joint on fire. I swear by all the saints.

At these words, the mule suddenly drops to its knees, the knees of its front legs, remains in that position for a moment, and then gets back on its feet.

ROBERTO: Come on, do something, you cowardly son of a bitch. You don't dare!

RAÚL: The chickens have mites; we don't want these filthy birds anymore.

CHAPARRO: We're going to send them to Heaven. Yes, by all the saints.

As if struck by lightning, the mule falls to its knees again. Now we realize that it must have been trained to fall to its knees on this cue. Jeers and shouts. Hombre shakes his chicken till its feathers fly.

HOMBRE: What does the chicken do after it lays its egg?

COCHINO: Yes, what does the chicken do after it lays its egg? If you come out, we'll tell you.

THE INMATES (in unison): What does the chicken do after it lays its egg? (Jeers and cheers.) It gets laid.

CHAPARRO: By all the saints!

The mule again falls obediently and almost mechanically to its knees, then struggles to its feet again.

LORENZO: By all the saints!

GUADALAJERO: Oh, what an innocent, pious little animal! By all the saints!

Twice in a row the mule falls to its knees, throws itself down, and is by now breathing hard. But the inmates give it no peace; they keep shouting the cue in wild confusion. The tormented mule keeps throwing itself down; it abrades its knees and groans.

THE INMATES (in unison): By all the saints! (then in wild confusion) By all the saints! By all the saints!

The mule is exhausted and confused by so many commands at once. It remains obediently kneeling, its hind legs upright, and does not get up anymore. It holds perfectly still except for a slight tremor in its scrawny flanks.

Up on the balcony a last chair is piled on top of the other objects. Then silence ensues. The two panels of the door remain open because the desk is still jammed there. In the meantime the room must have been completely emptied out, to judge by everything stacked on the balcony. Even the pictures have been removed from the walls and are lying in a pile on the whitewashed balustrade.

Down below the inmates are tormenting their screeching chickens in order to call attention to themselves once more. The mule remains kneeling, motionless. Terrible hooting.

ROBERTO: We're going to kill all the chickens!

LORENZO: We're getting them ready for the oven! We're going to toast the mites!

COCHINO: We're going to roast them right now and set the barn on fire.

HOMBRE: There's nothing like a nice little blaze! Let's go—to the barn!

COCHINO: Hand me the matches; we'll smoke him out.

The inmates rush to the barn, the chickens under their arms. Cochino lights an oil-soaked rag, which immediately begins to emit black smoke. But the inmates set fire only to some boards that the tractor tore off, which they stack up neatly a few steps from the barn. Apparently they do not dare to set the whole barn on fire. They toss several empty burlap bags into the flames that produce considerable smoke, which the wind drives along the front of the barn.

Alone in front of the administration building on the bare, deserted yard kneels the mule. Under the arcades Chicklets crouches, completely sunk into himself and motionless. Dust swirls, the wind whistles. For a few moments it is almost quiet.

Into the brief silence a terrible long drawn-out cry suddenly issues from the administration building, an appalling, marrow-piercing cry. This is real; it is Pepe's cry.

As if struck by lightning the inmates pause in what they are doing, almost incredulous. Startled, they let go of the chickens, which are promptly driven across the yard by the wind, their feathers fluffed. In frantic haste the inmates try to extinguish the fire, pulling the smoldering boards apart and throwing sand on them. All of a sudden the game is over, profound confusion; the performance comes to a crashing halt now that something has really happened.

The door flies open, the locked door of the administration building. The besieged preceptor storms out, his face terrifyingly distorted. The mule jumps up and flees. Chicklets still crouches there, oblivious. The preceptor storms past the barn as the inmates scatter. He runs out onto the field where the tractor disappeared. Out of his mind, he shouts as he passes the inmates.

PRECEPTOR: Victors! I see nothing but victors!

He storms to the fence, suddenly digs his heels into the ground; dust flies up from his ankles, swirls into the air, as the preceptor stops in his tracks. He jerks to a halt and remains standing by an old tree stump from which a single branch extends horizontally.

PRECEPTOR: You swine, put your arm down . . . stop pointing . . .
     this minute, I say . . . this minute, I say . . . stop pointing, I
     say . . . . All right, now I'm going to raise my hand, too, I'm going
     to point at you till you stop pointing . . . . I'm not going to stop
     till . . .

The preceptor raises his hand directly in front of the stump and, arm outstretched, begins to point at it.

PRECEPTOR: Stop pointing, I say . . . what a day . . . victory! The
     President awarded me both ears . . .

(All at once everything turns white, a gigantic bullfight arena filled with harsh white light. The sand is burning white in the sun. Cheers, the cheering of thousands of voices echoing hollowly through the rotunda. We see the bull, a mighty old bull with gray curls on his forehead between his horns and scrawny, sunken hindquarters. His flanks have spots where the coat has been rubbed off. The bull is mortally wounded, swaying slightly, but still standing. Now we see the torero, the preceptor in torero garb. In skintight, gold-embroidered knee breeches the dwarf stands beside the bull, leaning casually against him, and now the cheering grows even louder. The torero stands only as tall as the ridge of the bull's back. He is still holding the cape casually, and in the roar of applause he crosses his arms over his chest. His gold-embroidered jacket is also skintight, and above it is the rosy, wrinkled face; his short, crooked calves are hugged by white stockings. The bull trembles, and now the torero can allow himself everything, that is how excellent his coup de grâce was. With a bored air he leans against the animal's side and gazes at his fingernails. The mighty animal is losing urine, dribbling, a thin trickle. Now amid the frenetic cheering the torero grabs the tail of the still upright bull and begins to braid the switch. From the floor of the arena he calmly picks up a bottle of beer and takes a few swallows. The bull begins to wobble. Very harsh white light. The preceptor is recognizable again, standing by the horizontal branch, his hand raised, the finger pointing at it.)

(This dream sequence will presumably be cut.)

PRECEPTOR: Both ears! . . . pointed at me, you swine . . . . I'm not
    lowering my hand . . . I won't get tired, that would be ridicu-
    lous . . . . As long as you point at me, I'll point back, ha! My arm
    won't tire . . . gravity has become weaker, now leaves already fall
    upward . . . . There, over there, we have mist already . . . that's foli-
    age very high up and far away . . . . Today the leaves are rising . . .
    lower your finger, I can outlast you . . . my arm is very light . . .

The preceptor stands and stands there, keeping his arm unwaveringly outstretched and not allowing it to fall. He points

unwaveringly with his finger; dust swirls around him, billowing in plumes across the plain with the cacti. Up against the mountains the mist is cold and very white.

In the Police Lockup

The last image, a long, patient shot, remaining unchanged for many minutes. An almost bare room in a police lockup with only the most meager furnishings: a desk, a chair, a bench, a few photos on the wall, file cases. The window is half-barred, and we can see through the open window a wall that encloses a courtyard. In the middle of the room is a tripod holding a rather old-fashioned camera. Facing it, pushed almost to the wall, is a stool with a thin iron rod in lieu of a backrest. Chaparro is seated on the stool, his right hand calmly holding at chest height a metal tag bearing a number. A police photographer is fussing with the camera. He has tossed his uniform jacket over the back of the chair behind his desk, and his shirt has sweat stains in the armpits. From his broad leather belt hangs a holster with a revolver. The barrel of the revolver extends almost down to his ankle. Chaparro wriggles forward on the stool and jumps off, looking uncertain.

PHOTOGRAPHER (curtly): Stop! Get back on . . . we're nowhere near finished.

Chaparro scrambles back onto the stool he left prematurely; he pulls himself up, knee first. Then he turns with some difficulty to face the camera.

PHOTOGRAPHER: Lean back, lean your head back . . . just your head. The number higher . . . higher. All right, now turn your head to the left . . . look at the door handle . . . hold still . . .

Chaparro carries out the orders patiently, turns his head to the left and focuses on the door handle. The officer climbs on a footstool to be able to look into the viewfinder and snaps the picture.

PHOTOGRAPHER: The number higher, don't keep letting it drop. The number has to show in the picture . . . . All right, now turn your head to the right; we need to get the left ear . . . . Farther . . . farther . . . even farther . . . look at the window. All right, now lean your head back with the other ear against the rod and don't move . . .

Chaparro leans his head as ordered and holds perfectly still. The officer mounts the footstool again and snaps the photo. Chaparro remains motionless in position.

PHOTOGRAPHER: Now one more from the front. Hey there . . .

Chaparro gazes absentmindedly out the window; he moves his head, which was leaning with the right ear against the iron rod, slightly forward and rubs his ear, looking unwaveringly out the window.

CHAPARRO: I heard ringing in my ear. That means someone's thinking of me.

The camera pans very, very slowly and carefully away from Chaparro and follows his gaze, traveling cautiously toward the window. A long, long, long fixed gaze out the window; that is the final image. A bleak courtyard enclosed by a high wall, a bit of sparse, dried-up, sandy lawn, a sandstrewn path, a bench. Beyond that, far in the distance, a few wretched Mexican suburban houses; barren land, a construction site with no one working, a dried-up cement mixer. Nothing stirs for the length of several minutes. For a while one still faintly hears instructions being given in the next room. We see only bleakness, unchanging. Now, very far off, an emaciated stray dog ambles by. Then for a long time nothing again, not a human soul. Then a sparrow, a sparrow flies onto the courtyard wall. The sparrow becomes the major event. It flutters off. A long, long gaze out the window.

Fata Morgana

I. The Creation

SPEAKER: And it is told how once the earth swayed in deep quiet, swayed in deep silence, rested in stillness, softly rocking, and lay there, lonely and void.

And this is the first testimony, the first word.

There was no man, nor beast, fowl, fish, crab, tree, stone, cave, gorge, grass-tuft, nor bush; only the heavens were there. Invisible was the face of the earth, only the seas gathered under the firmament, that was all.

Nothing was there to take form or become audible, nothing to move, trickle, or rush under the firmament. There was only the nothingness.

Only the creatress was there and the creator, it was She, the Mighty, and Cucumatz, Herself, the child-bearer, and the begetter of sons were there upon the unfathomable waters. Omniscient and omnipotent was their essence. And likewise there truly was heaven, and also the "Heart of Heaven": this is the name of the God, this is how He is named.

And his word came thither, unto the Mighty and to Cucumatz, where there was darkness and night, and talked to the Mighty and to Cucumatz. And they talked and bethought themselves and considered carefully, took council among themselves and brought their words and considerations into accord.

There emerged from their plans the dawning of light and the conception of man.

And then they pondered the sprouting, the growing of trees and creepers, the springing up of life, and the creation of mankind in darkness and night, on the strength of Him, who is the "Heart of Heaven," and whose name is Huracan: Huracan-flash-of-lightning is his first appearance, the second is Tom-thumb-lightning, the third, at last, is green-lightning—by these three is the "Heart of Heaven" encompassed.

And they came to the Mighty and to Cucumatz and considered light and life: "In what manner shall life be sown and how shall light shine? Who shall be our ward and keeper? O that it may come to pass! This thou shalt ponder! Recede o ye waters, abate ye from the earth! For there is no splendor nor renown, nor glory in this, our work, our creation, lest man be built, man be created." Thus spake they.

And earth was created by them. Yes, indeed, thus it came forth. So that earth might come forth, they said, "Earth," and it at once appeared. Merely like a cloud, like unto a haze when it first took shape, in its first manifestation. Then the mountains were heard rising out of the waters, and they were majestic instanter.

And Cucumatz rejoiced: "It was good that thou camest down unto us, thou 'Heart of Heaven,' thou Huracan, thou Tom-thumb-lightning, thou green-lightning!" "Our creation and our work will be well-made," spake they.

Earth, the mountains, the plains thus came forth. And everywhere the courses of the rivers were set: they meandered and wound at the foot of the mountains and between them. Well parted the rivers were, after the high mountains had come forth into light. Thus came this earth into being.

And further, they now thought out the beasts of the mountains, the keepers of all forests, the inhabitants of the mountains: the stag, fowl, puma, and jaguar, the snake, rattlesnake, and viper, the wards of the creepers.

And the child-bearer and the begetter of sons spake: "Shall it be all void, shall it be all still under the trees and creepers? Would not it be wise now to have somebody watch over them?" spake they, bethinking themselves and taking council the one with the other.

At once the stag and the fowl were shaped, and now they showed the stag and the fowl their habitation: "Thou, stag, shalt sleep near the course of the river, in the gorges, here thou shalt dwell, betwixt grass-bushels and herbs. In the forests shalt thou multiply! Let it be so!" they said unto them.

Then the small birds and the big birds received their abode: "Ye birds of the treetops and the creepers, may ye dwell and nest here! Here may ye breed and multiply on the branches of the trees, and on the tendrils and creepers."

Thus was the earth haunted by them, and each was given his bed and his resting place. In this manner the child-bearer and the begetter of sons gave the beasts of the earth their habitation—thus all the stags and fowl became alive.

And the stags and fowl were told by the creatress and the creator, by the child-bearer and the begetter of sons: "Speak orderly, do not clamor or shout without sense, speak coherently, everyone in his manner, everyone after his family, everyone after his kind."

However, it came to pass that they spake not as human beings would . . .

When the creatress and the creator heard that they failed to speak as human beings do, they said to each other: "They have not in the least mastered the calling of our names, although we are their constructors and their creators. That is not in order."

Therefore the creatress and the creator essayed once more to build living beings, to make moving creatures. "Without fail let us try anew!"

Time drew near for the dissemination of man and for the illumination. "Let us build ourselves a keeper!"

The flesh of man was made of tzite wood, but when woman was carved by the creatress and the creator, the flesh of woman was made of reed-grass marrow.

But still the creatures were without sense, they spake not before the face of their creatress and their creator, who made them, who formed them.

And so were they destroyed, drowned.

For their sakes, the face of the earth was darkened; there reigned a rain-darkness, pelting rain by day, and pelting rain by night. Small beasts and big beasts flocked together. Trees and rocks cried shame upon them.

They determined to climb up the huts, but the huts made them tumble, and they fell. They determined to climb the trees, but they were cast off by the trees. They determined to hide in the caves, but the caves closed before them.

In this manner the second destruction of the beings formed or created like man took place, of the beings that are doomed to perish, to fall. They were extinguished, they were all, root and branch, destroyed.

II. Paradise

SPEAKER: Now "Flying Robert" appears small at the horizon, umbrella in hand, his hair teased by the wind, wet through and shaken, rigid and sad like no other.

In Paradise you cross the sand without seeing your shadow. There is landscape even without deeper meaning. Paradise is available to everybody. In Paradise only God is looking on. There you cross the sand without seeing your face. There is landscape even without deeper meaning. The gates of Paradise are open to everybody. There, works are inspected that no one would do. There you dig holes without stumbling on man. There you slake lime and are chosen for this task by the rich. There men cast a shadow in spite of the scorching sun. Afterward rare animals were seen there.

MAN WITH LIZARD: I have but sixteen years left to investigate how these lizards can bear the glowing heat of this sun here, and even find nourishment. They live on the few existing creatures in this desert, smaller lizards and mice, which are hidden away in sand holes during the day.

Otherwise they are real carnivorous animals; you can see it here, the many flies which have gathered here.

MAN WITH THE LETTER: I have been away from Germany fifteen years.

"Dear Eugen, we received your letter very much. How are you? Are you in the hot countries? How are you? Isn't it too warm at your place? And when are you coming back?" Yes, I'm coming back.

BOY: One dinar, one dinar, one dinar . . .

MAN WITH THE LETTER: Five marks, or nothing at all.

MAN WITH LIZARD: Yes, there are certain kinds of animal, like fat-tail sheep, on which we depend a lot. They too can bear such terrific temperatures of about fifty or sixty degrees centigrade. But there are only a few. A few birds move up into the air, thus cooling themselves off. But apart from those, there is scarcely anything living to be found.

The desert doesn't make it very easy for us to catch these animals. For days one has to march across dunes and through wind in order to come across the lizards. Individual animals run away at a terrific speed and try to save themselves in their holes. But then you have to dig them up with a spade in this heat. That's no pleasure. But you can imagine to what trouble one will go to learn about the life of these animals.

SPEAKER: In Paradise, roasted pigeons fly directly into your mouth. There you enjoy yourself without being forced to. There enjoyment means obligation.

GIRL: The "blitzkrieg" is madness, etc.

SPEAKER: In Paradise even Gentiles move mountains. There wars are prevented by mothers. There you expect herons from the left. In Paradise ruins mean happiness. There you find gates without borders.

In Paradise plane wrecks have been distributed in the desert in advance. There the landscape is as God has commanded it to be.

In Paradise you call "Hallo" without seeing anybody. There you quarrel with strangers to avoid having friends. In Paradise man is born dead.

While you are sleeping, acids gnaw and leeches suck at the tunafish.

While you are dreaming, an apple from a tree falls onto your brow.

While you are waiting, trains break in two, you breathe softly, as though you were dead.

While you recline, carelessly strewn stars look out into space.

While you are sleeping, God softly walks over the fields with Maria.

III. The Golden Age

SPEAKER: In the Golden Age man and wife live in harmony. Now, for example, they appear before the lens of the camera, death in their eyes, a smile on their faces, a finger in the pie. Running, they train themselves harder and harder. Weightlifting too is rewarding.

Unforgettable, however, remains a jump from the lighthouse. In the Golden Age traces of Paradise can still be discerned. Here, for example, a boat once landed. Furiously the waves beat against the shore. In the background, smoke is rising—that is to say, not even worse than you expected. Stones that were cast do not return by themselves.

In the Golden Age man does not forget to pray, lest God's end be uncomely.

More than by death, even, blessings, and curses, man is disturbed by smoke over the world.

Beneath the earth the children have found a fire. And now the parents wish suddenly to return to houses of stone. That's enough, even one of these thoughts would have done.

MAN IN THE LAVA: And yet from this mysterious soil they wrestle harvests, the reaping of which gives part pain to the farmer and part pleasure. It is difficult not to come across a dromedary at the wayside, typically bridled as draught-working-pack-and-saddle-animal.

ENGLISH TOURIST: Ah yes, saddle-animal . . .

MAN IN THE LAVA: And here, scarcely have we turned our eyes to the right, the rapture is over again for the visitor. The sight is terrifying. Silence is needed. Calmly we ask ourselves, where are we going? And silence is almost the answer.

We glide over the landscape, and it seems as though this tragic vision would be unending, full of a strange beauty, otherwise hellish. Our eyes cannot stand this for very long, and an inner voice urges us to hurry on and look at the powerful growth of the plants, which are wrestled from the hot soil.

MAN WITH THE TURTLE: What can we learn about the turtle? For it has four flippers, with which it moves forward; it has a solid shell, it also has a solid belly. Here it has its head with the mouth where it takes nourishment. It also has a behind, where it comes out again. Now I'm going to get it once more.

SPEAKER: There is nothing like the Peace of the Golden Age,
War is proclaimed dead by Peace.
Nothing is great as the sand,
Nothing is great as the Peace.
The land is entranced with Peace.

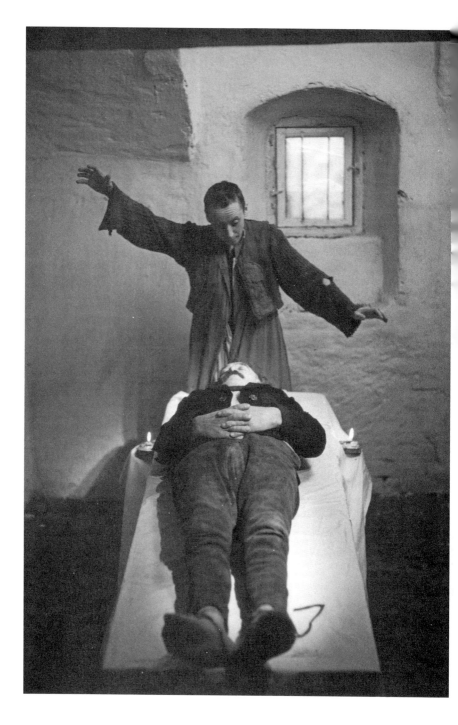

Heart of Glass

The Scenario: A Summary

The inventor of Ruby glass has died with his secret. After a master glassblower's unsuccessful effort to produce this magical glass, the owner of the glass factory tries to find the secret by scouring old books, but to no avail. Next he sends for the shepherd, Hias, who is known for his prophetic gifts. The factory owner presses Hias for the precious information, but he fails to get it.

Madness speaks out of the factory owner when he proclaims that he is in possession of the secret. The people willingly believe him, for among the glassblowers, madness is rampant.

The factory owner determines that the blood of a virgin is essential to the formula for Ruby glass. He stabs his servant girl—Hias's girlfriend—in a ritual accompanied by music from a harp. As always, he is aided by his aged servant, Adalbert.

Meanwhile, a euphoric celebration ensues at the inn. Hias is haunted by a vision of the future that breaks out of him. As long as the vision lasts, nothing at all can interrupt it. Although the Fool dances naked on his table, and the glass factory erupts in flames by the hand of the factory owner himself, and the news of his girlfriend's gruesome murder arrives, Hias's vision unfolds intact.

The glassblowers search for a culprit, and they mistake the prediction of evil with its origin. Hias is delivered up to justice.

Via Mala

There is a somber fog, which gradually dissolves: now we behold the most dismal abyss of all. The craggy walls decline dramatically, and, down there, the panic of death is crouching. The rocks exhale a wet coldness. At a point where you can discern a piece of the horizon, two old stone bridges arch across the void; they stand at a nearly imperceptible angle against each other. Why there are two bridges remains a mystery.

In the foreground we notice Hias, sitting heavily on a stone terrace, almost in the pit of the abyss, brooding. We realize that he has been sunken in brooding for hours. Hias is stout and heavy, possessing enormous physical strength, but everything about him seems to be of an introverted nature. His heavily inclined torso rests on an elbow, which he supports on his knee.

And now we realize that something is stirring inside him. His hands move slightly, like gestures in an imaginary conversation; his gaze is completely away and adrift in dream. A spell passes over his big, heavy-boned farmer's face.

HIAS: Come over—come!

He doesn't turn; throughout the scene he will not turn around. His gaze persists in the imaginary.

HIAS: Come down, I said!

To the side, behind him, where the stone-hewn steps of the path lead down into the abyss, down to Hias, four timid farmers appear from behind a rock. As none of them dares to be first, they are shoving themselves along. Their hats are drawn; respectfully they stand two steps behind Hias in a posture of devotion. The farmers are very poor and awkward fellows, and we can guess that they are dressed in their Sunday clothes. Hias, who is conscious of the four behind him, keeps staring straight ahead.

HIAS: So, what?

The farmers shove one man in front, who seems to be their appointed speaker. After some hesitation, it bursts out of him:

FARMER: The village lives in fear. Ruepp says he's seen a Giant. The time of the Giants is coming back.

A second farmer musters some courage.

SECOND FARMER: The Giant breaks the trees and beats our cattle. He tears out our bowels whenever he sees us.

The stupid young farmer with a sheep's face steps forward.

YOUNG FARMER: He is licking our brains out.

Hias has listened, motionless, without turning toward the four. He is struck by enlightenment.

HIAS: Tell Ruepp that there is no Giant. Next time he should pay attention to the angle of the sun. The sun had set; the Giant was just the shadow of a dwarf.

The four farmers are overcome by ineffable happiness.

HIAS: And I'll tell you something else. Look up at the bridges. One shall soon be crossed by a liar and the other by a thief.

At the nauseating height we observe the bridges. Over one of them a spectral figure with a long black billowing cape hastens along, loping like the villain in a play; a breath later, a second one crosses the other bridge, likewise a gloomy figure.

We see Hias closely as he is overcome by a deep trance. The farmers turn around in dumb happiness, and they withdraw with maniacally hollow and rhythmic steps, as if they were folk dancing.

HIAS: If nothing changes, take that as a blessing. But I see something with the glass factory coming on.

The farmers stop listening. They stomp the rocky ground with their feet.

Suddenly music swells up, in the same precise rhythm in which the farmers move. The rocks cry out a twofold echo toward the men—yodeling sounds in the damp-chilled chasm.

The music grows louder. We see the bridges against the sky, and on one of them a procession of farmers moves with ecstatic spasms and with the same dancing steps. The flag carried in front swings rhythmically in the air.

Superimposed across the procession, at the nauseating height and against the dismal sky, we see the opening tides. Then night falls into the abyss.

On the Falkenstein

An iris, as in old silents, and the image unravels with light. But we know that night is falling once again.

Hias sits on a rock on the Falkenstein, gazing over the landscape in trance, dream-lost. Over Mount Rachel opposite him, the sun drops, huge and heavy. With a sluggish heat of his wings, the last raven passes, seeking shelter for the night.

HIAS: I see fire flowing in the brook and the wind pushing the fire on, and I see trees burn like matches. I see many people running up a hill; they stop on the hilltop, breathless and paralyzed; they turn to stone. One beside the other, a whole forest of stone. Then it gets dark and quiet, and I see that down below everything has perished, no living being is left and no house, just some debris. It is rigidly and deathly quiet. Yes, and then I see someone running on Waldhausstrasse with a burning branch in his hand, screaming, "Am I really the only one? Am I really the last?"

Hias breathes heavily while peering into the imaginary. Slow music ensues. Mist and the quavering sun above Mount Rachel sink lower. The images emerge from the mist.

Visions

Above the wooded hills, fogs and clouds are spreading swiftly. They hover and wallow; the clouds speed on as fast as a train. The wooded countryside is sprawled, alien and flickering.

VOICE OF HIAS: I see how it shall be just before the end. The last birds can't find the ground anymore. The soil has drowned.

We are looking at a rocky tower, erect like a pillow in the rain-veiled foam of the sea. Around it, white birds are circling; they settle; they start circling again.

VOICE OF HIAS: When the rock itself disappears, there will be no place left to sit on, only water. I see some pushing. I can see so many birds at once.

The Islas Guaneras. Several black islands in the ocean. When we look closer, we discover that these are not islands but unimaginable numbers of guano birds heaped on top of each other in the sea. Settlements of millions upon millions of birds.

A rock that is one of these "islands" is no longer visible. The sea is sullen, almost black; there are no waves but rather furrows, like the skin of a horse when jerking to chase off a horsefly.

VOICE OF HIAS: A rider goes over a beach, but I don't know where: a beach beyond comparison. The rider is galloping away from us. He is chasing whole clouds of silver-white birds, which turn about in the sky in gigantic hordes. Now the whole sky is silvery with them; now they change direction, and all is gray. It is like billions of insects above the reed grass. It all begins when the reverend gentlemen start beating each other. I can see two adversary priests rowing on Lake Arber.

We look at Lake Arber, its water lying still like a black mirror. From different directions, the priests row toward each other. They meet at the middle of the lake and start beating each other in terribly slow and laborious movements. They swing their oars over their heads. Both wear gowns and big hats, like the priests in Italy.

VOICE OF HIAS: The trees are beginning to fall, and a burning cow gallops through the woods. In the forest, a large, aching fir tree sways to one side and falls to the ground. It crashes down with a hollow sound and swings up again. The sound of the crash is accompanied by the aching of another fir tree that swoons and falls nearby. With one vehement stroke, an entire stretch of forest collapses, from the Forlorn Bluff to the depths of the woods.

Hias's voice is no longer audible; it drowns. We see an entire orchestra playing imaginary instruments. From the dimness, the visage of an infant flickers into form; it clings so firmly to a clothesline that it stays there, hanging on its own. We see that the baby is crying, but we don't hear it because of the music.

We see a long line of paralyzed hens, one behind the other, beaks to the ground, all the way down a hall and out the door. The hens keep still, breathing heavily.

A dog is standing in the room like a statue and doesn't move from its spot, trembling almost imperceptibly. Slowly the images become more intimate to our experience, but they remain all the more mysterious.

We are looking through an open door into a room, where some sort of drama is taking place, but we see just half of the room; the other half remains an enigma. People are moving around a table; they disappear; for a long spell, nothing; then, a woman flees out the door, panic-stricken. Then the door is locked from inside. We are left outside the neglected house, a short rattle from the doorknob.

From out of a window, a strange sight. Through flakes of slow-falling snow, we see a beach, and beyond it the rolling surf. It is a sad, mournful picture: it is a Gloom.

We have another flickering view through a second window of the somber scene outside. There, snowflakes are falling and sinking, and behind, a massive waterfall, like the waterfall of the

Rhine. The flakes are falling and falling; the waters rush more and more.

After a lengthy gaze, the snow and water seem to come to a halt, and an odd sensation sets in: we are moving upward with the room. It is like staring at a brook from a bridge or like being on a train, when through the window the world seems to be moving, though it's actually the train that moves. The images flicker and fade away; stillness reigns. Above Mount Rachel, the sun sinks in the mist, glowing red.

Now we see Hias staring at the last crescent of the fireball, in total trance.

HIAS: The sun stings. And next, someone sets fire to the glass factory. The factories burn because they have come to an end.

The picture fades.

Cemetery

Unfolding from a distant point, the image rests in itself.

We see a newly made grave. Wreaths that have hardly started to dry in the wind. Few sounds from the village. Two magpies are quarreling. We feel that we are back with the action. At the right corner of the grave, Mother Anamirl, a little old woman with a face like a leathery apple that has passed the winter on a shelf. She is dressed in faded black. Kneeling, she prays with deep devotion, as in Manneristic paintings of the early Renaissance.

The sun is shining.

No background.

Mansion

The factory owner is sitting in an easy chair by candlelight, wearing a ruffled shirt that is open at the throat. Before him is a ruby-red mug, half-filled with wine, and the burning candle. He stares hypnotically upon the glowing mug, and we realize that it must be made of particularly valuable glass. Behind and to the right of the easy chair is a fireplace with a feeble fire.

The factory owner rubs his heart slowly, over and over.

Gradually the picture unravels with light; then the circle diminishes down to a point. The final thing our eyes rest upon, precisely in the center of the picture, is the mug of Ruby glass.

Inn

A simple, ample chamber. Heavy wooden boards on the floor, which are very light in color from too much cleansing. Several long rough wooden tables without backrests. In the background, the counter; on the side, some beer barrels. On the wall, a small blackboard scribbled with chalk, as if for bowling. Few patrons. Silence reigns amid the beer drinking.

The inn is rustic, but without all the attributes of the *rustic* as seen today in inns with an artificially backwoods touch.

The room on the whole gives an impression of scantiness and has a taste of the customers' poverty. At one of the tables, Wudy and Ascherl sit opposite one another, holding beers. It is evening; a candle flickers on the table. Both men are mute.

They stare at each other. They look through one another as if they were looking through glass.

WUDY: It will all be over for you tomorrow, Ascherl.

Ascherl waits; it is slowly sinking in. Wudy empties his stein.

WUDY: And I am going to sleep this drink off over your corpse.

Ascherl peeks out from his deep absentmindedness for a moment.

ASCHERL: Hey, master—bring Wudy another beer!
WUDY: I shall sleep on your corpse.

The innkeeper shuffles over and takes the empty mug. Wudy squirms heavily in his chair; his tongue weighs tons.

WUDY: Hias has said that I'll sleep on your corpse. Hias sees the future.

ASCHERL: On the condition that I'll sleep in the hay. And first I would have to fall down on the threshing floor. And then you would have to fall on top of me; it will be over for you, too, if you don't fall softly.

The innkeeper brings the fresh stein of beer. Wudy positions it exactly on the watery circle left by the previous one.

WUDY: You'll be done for, and I'll sleep.

Ascherl drinks. He is so far away nothing can reach him anymore. Wudy broods.

WUDY: That's it.

Glass Factory

A cavernous, hall-like chamber, in the center of which the round furnace is set. The furnace stands on a round brick platform that is scarcely one meter high. On this platform the glassblowers work all around the furnace. About forty men have room to work there. The furnace itself is circular with a slight hump, a little taller than a man; nine openings are posited in its circle, from which the liquid glass is withdrawn. Movable shields have been placed near the openings to protect the glassblowers from the heat. In the furnace there is such an unimaginable heat that a blinding glare leaps from the glowing holes.

On the edge of the platform—that is to say, a bit farther below— the hands are working. There are different wooden molds that can be opened, and they are filled by the glassblowers with a molten lump. Also, water basins made of tin for cooling. The hands wear heavy leather gloves.

At the edge of the platform, beer mugs are all around. The heat is tremendous. There is continuous drinking. The men are wearing leather aprons.

In the background, leaning against the wall at a right angle, is a cooling furnace with two holes. The newly made pieces are put into the furnace to be cooled off slowly for hours. Usually, there is a constant coming and going between the two furnaces.

We see the hall, the furnace, the men. Hardly any movement; a great Paralysis seems to have overcome them.

In one of the glowing holes, the fire minder, Agide, slowly inserts log after log. We realize it is senseless work. The workmen don't work—they brood. They brood in postures of brooding. The flames blaze from the furnace.

Agide keeps tending the fire. Against the glow, he is as black as a paper silhouette.

The glow radiates from out of the picture.

To the side, the melter, Wenzel, broods in a brain-racked posture and stares at the floor. Agide sits beside him. He carries the last log in his hands.

AGIDE: He did know how to write.

Wenzel doesn't move. He sits like a statue.

AGIDE: He could have written that down easily—

Wenzel, as if made of ore, begins to stir.

Having come back to life, he fumbles for his beer stein and drinks. He wipes off his mouth.

AGIDE: —how the Ruby glass is made.
WENZEL: Have you ever written a word yourself?
AGIDE: But he could have talked, that Muehlbeck.
WENZEL: Try to get a word from a dead man.

The men become mute, the Paralysis overcoming them, as they grow into marble and ore.

Inn

At the inn, Wudy and Asherl still sit facing each other. For a long time they gaze at each other torpidly. Apparently, they've just quarreled, and neither knows what to say. Full of animosity, they stare through one another. Ascherl reaches for his beer mug, raises it slowly, and conks it on Wudy's head, sending glass shards flying. Wudy remains sitting, motionless. The mug has crashed on him as if on stone. He looks at Ascherl as if he were dreaming. Ascherl, too, studies Wudy as in a dream. Long inertia. Delirious, Wudy lifts his fist and across the table punches Ascherl. Wudy has knocked over his stein. With great care, Ascherl seizes Wudy, who is leaning over the table with the upper half of his body.

The innkeeper comes up from the side and grabs the two by their hair.

INNKEEPER: Break it up. Go sleep off your drink in the hay.

He pulls the men up. Seen from the table, the innkeeper shoves the two past the counter and out the door.

Paulin's Room

The room is poor and bare, like a convent's. But across the floor and over the table and chair, untidiness is spreading, which is oddly produced with only a few pieces of clothes, dirty wash, and some senseless haberdashery.

A bed, lengthwise, where Paulin sleeps. Her mattress is stuffed with dried bracken.

Knocking on the door. Paulin groans. The shout "Paulin!" from the hostess. Paulin tries to rise on all fours in her bed. Door opening, footsteps. The hostess is coming to the bedside. She draws off the blanket with a single yank.

HOSTESS: Lying in bed naked again.

She slaps Paulin's behind.

Paulin, confused and senseless, struggles out of bed.

HOSTESS: Get dressed.

The hostess leaves. Paulin reaches for her dress on the floor.

Mansion

We see two regal rooms, which are adjoined. Choice furniture, exquisite china in a glass display case, and in another display, reddish glass. Paintings and heavy carpets. In the first room, a slender tiled stove from the Rococo era, with the tiles of the blackest ebony. It rests on graceful legs. At first glance, the rooms give an impression of nobility.

In the room reigns an unearthly silence and emptiness.

A closed door.

The door handle is pressed down. The door opens. The glass factory owner enters. With exaggerated slowness, he steps to the center of the room and remains standing on the carpet. He listens into himself.

FACTORY OWNER: Adalbert!

He leaves, drifts out the door. A strange scene, like someone who has lost himself on the stage. We look at the door, which has been left open. From outside, we hear the factory owner shouting "Adalbert!" again.

Village

Some poor houses lie there; they lie there, dead. Rain has fallen, cold and autumnal. From the chimneys, smoke is rising; it hovers, immobile, at the height of the roofs in the wet air.

A house from its side. Agide is standing under a window, hammering away on a piece of beech wood that has been cut flat like a shelf. Agide has the log attached to a rope, which is fixed around the center of the length of wood. He hammers it with a wooden mallet in different places so that distinct sounds are produced. When repeated, the sounds result in a kind of signal.

Agide beats the beech board as if it were the Great Music.

Mansion

Adalbert, plump and sentimental like a pastry baker, dresses the owner of the glass factory as if he were a nobleman of the Century of the Braid. He adorns him high and low for a scene of celebration. Finally, the factory owner equips himself and puts his hat on. Adalbert slowly opens the glass door to the balcony, which looks upon a small overgrown park, and he steps out into it.

Following his gaze, we behold Mount Rachel, beyond the park, where the sun is just now rising. We hear Agide's signal whirring through the air. In the villages, doors are slammed.

Adalbert opens the door to find the maid, Ludmilla, with the breakfast tray. She is very young and as pale as wax, like a girl afflicted with anemia. Her hair is brushed back unbecomingly and tied in a knot. Behind her frailty, something of a backwoods Madonna radiates out.

ADALBERT: My gracious lord does not want to have breakfast now.

From the background comes the factory owner's voice.

VOICE OF FACTORY OWNER: Ludmilla may wear her hair down today.
ADALBERT: (condescendingly) An honor for the servant girl.

Ludmilla hesitates at first, then retreats. Adalbert closes the door.

The closed door.

Swamp

The Forlorn Bluff. On the crest of the Bavarian Woods, there is a nearly open space with some reed grass, which is bordered by dark fir trees on all sides. Like monstrous corpses of trees, enormous beeches lie prostrate on the ground and molder in the bog. Lichen grows over the rotting wood. Some stand far away from each other in loneliness. One is bare; it has been split from top to bottom by lightning. The landscape is primeval, one in which dinosaurs might live.

Parts of the high plain have turned into swamps, with flowering moss and, every now and then, round waterholes, like eyes emerging from the darkest Dark. From the forest, a hush blows over. We can gaze far into the Bavarian Woods. Hillcrest after hillcrest and woodland after woodland—all are of a deep darkness. A great quiet over the treetops. Hias crosses the bog, sloshing, swaggering. He pauses.

HIAS: Moooo—

He listens.

HIAS: Moooo—

Hias advances a few steps and spots the bull he has been looking for. He attaches a little bell around the calm beast's neck. Hias goes first; the bull follows him. The bull sinks in the boggy mud almost up to his back, but he moves on. The bell is jangling. They disappear into the woods. A cold autumn fog draws near.

Village

The village is awake now. Something is going to happen. Women are peeking discreetly from the windows. On the clay road, many people are moving diagonally, to the left. The glass factory owner is proceeding forth in a grandiose state. There is some strange enchantment lying over the people. Some move ahead in dancing, stamping steps. It is like a religious trance, just before the end of a pilgrimage.

Behind the factory owner, crippled people dribble in pursuit.

We can hear Paulin's cry. The cripples come to a halt, glance at each other, and move on.

Barn

Paulin stands with a pitchfork on the threshing floor, staring straight ahead. Abruptly, she erupts with a mad cry that emits from her bewildered brain.

Now we realize that, at her feet, Wudy and Ascherl are entwined in a lifeless tangle.

In one wing of the huge barn door, the hostess appears.

HOSTESS: What are you screaming about?

She catches sight of the flopped, limp duo.

HOSTESS: My God!

She makes the sign of the cross.

Glass Factory

The glassblower Gigl is a man with the chest of a bull, his face glistening with grease in the heat of the furnace. This is his hour, this is his scene—he is aware of his importance.

A large crowd of townspeople, glassblowers, farmhands, and even farmer's boys and lumberjacks surround him in heightened expectation. The glass factory owner is among them; respectfully the crowd keeps him at a distance. Adalbert pushes forward slightly.

ADALBERT: Isn't he wrong? Does he really have Ruby glass?

Gigl is so sure that, without giving an answer, he takes a big lump of white, glowing glass from the furnace with the aid of his glass pipe. He takes a deep breath so that his chest expands, places the pipe in his mouth, and begins to blow the molten glass into form using nothing but his hands.

The farmhand beside him nervously opens the wooden mold and causes a rattle amid the breathless silence.

Gigl shows that he is a true master. He lets the pipe, with

its glowing molten lump of glass, dance with the wondrous and knowing movements of his palms. During the process, he is always faster than the inclination of the glass to drip down to the floor. Masterly Gigl plays against the will of the molten, whitish, glowing matter. He blows a gigantic breath into the glass and puffs a balloon out of it all at once, a balloon as big as a man's skull.

The glass cools off and begins to show some color. Gigl is holding the balloon, which deftly he sets into large circular movements, first against his apron and then against the white glow of the furnace.

The glass has an opaque brownish hue.

The factory owner, who is closest to the object, is so dumbfounded that he makes some downward pumping gestures with his arms, as if he were pumping air into himself. Bending over, when he reaches his shoe tops, he roars.

FACTORY OWNER: No!

He draws the sword and gives the glass a blow. The glass balloon is still soft and sticks to the blade. The factory owner cannot shake it off; he throws the sword to the ground.

Abruptly he turns and moves away with wild steps. Only Adalbert follows him. The others remain motionless, a tableau of petrified horror.

Forest

The herdsman Sam, a lean, elderly day laborer, disappears behind some bulls' asses into the woods. He and his cattle are driven off by a bear's distinct grumble.

Sam is approached by Hias, who is trotting just like a bear while giving out bear sounds. When Hias is one step behind Sam, Sam raises his arm in the air and abruptly turns around, ducking down while drawing out his knife. He thrusts it into the upper arm of the imaginary bear. Both are very theatrical, as if partaking in a stage scene.

Hias roars with pain and drops down, as one would on a stage. Now the bull with the bell appears. He sniffs at Hias, who lies in the bracken.

Office

A large, dusty room, almost bare of furniture. The parquet floor is so dried up that it is full of crannies and groans beneath one's feet. Some bookshelves crammed with old, yellowed files packed in bundles. On one of the walls, a sofa and an easy chair, both covered with white linen. On the wall opposite, a mirror taller than a man, partly covered, as if blindfolded. Next to it, a display case holding precious samples of Ruby glass. Near the window, which forms a small bay, a desk.

The glass factory owner stands before the display case. He wears no overcoat and seems beset by bad dreams.

FACTORY OWNER: Adalbert!

Adalbert is on the spot at once and bows.

FACTORY OWNER: Send for the shepherd Hias to come here at once, so he may gaze upon the mystery of Ruby glass. And, if need be, let us tear Muehlbeck out of his grave again so that Hias can read from his brain.

Adalbert withdraws without a sound. We only hear the groaning of the planks.

The factory owner, near. He opens the case and removes the holy shrine: a mug, copper red.

FACTORY OWNER: My God, that was the second glass! And this glory will now be extinguished and vanish from the face of the earth. What will protect me from now on against the evil forces of the free universe?

He collapses as if stricken by a secret power.

Forest

Sam creeps out of a bark hut, ass first. In front of the hut, a newly made fire; beside it, Hias sits. Sam brings over some rags to bandage Hias's arm. Hias makes a face of severe pain. They utter their words like spoken law.

SAM: You're making a face like Paulin's.

HIAS: You've taken me for a bear.

SAM: The bulls have run away.

HIAS: I had the bear's feeling.

SAM: Go down to the master, who shall send us a hunter with a rifle. He shall burn the bear. And you bring me some flour.

Silence hovers between them.

Barn

Ascherl and Wudy lie on the threshing floor. Behind them, the innkeeper and his wife stand, not knowing what to do. Both speak into the void, estranged, as if an imaginary third person they have argued with were in the room.

INNKEEPER: They say Wudy is done for. He took me by the hair once and threw me on the ground, making my eye bleed.

HOSTESS: But it's Ascherl that's done for, because he called me a whore once, that old glutton. His evil mouth has been punished for lying.

She slaps the face of the man lying underneath.

INNKEEPER: Are you crazy? Do you want to kill him off?

HOSTESS: A whore calls for a good slapping.

INNKEEPER: He wanted to prove your whore's tricks.

HOSTESS: That's why he's done for now.

INNKEEPER: No, it's Wudy who is finished.

HOSTESS: Just look who's lying underneath. The one underneath is finished, which Hias predicted. Underneath is Ascherl.

The innkeeper musters courage and picks the two up. He puts Wudy and Ascherl side by side. He tests them by lifting an arm of each and letting them drop. The arms flop down heavily.

INNKEEPER: For heaven's sakes! I can't even tell who the dead one is by looking closely.

The innkeeper's wife flares up at the void.

HOSTESS: You don't curse a dead man in the face.

She turns away.
The innkeeper pinches them timidly. They lie as if dead.

Office

On the desk near the bay window, two untidy stacks of books are piled up. We know by the thickness of the tomes that they must be encyclopedias and dictionaries.

The factory owner has buried his head between two piles of books, and he skims down a page with his index finger.

FACTORY OWNER: Ru . . . Ru . . . Ru . . . Ru . . . Ru . . . Rubel. Nothing.

He closes the book, puts it on the left stack, and takes a new one from the right stack. He opens it and leafs through it, just as he did before.

FACTORY OWNER: Ru . . . Ru . . . Ru . . . Ru . . . Ruby. Nothing here either.

We see the book closely. It is turned upside down, but the words are right side up.

All this time, something like restless despair emanates from the factory owner.

Forest

It is a deeply primordial stretch of woods. Dark forest and high bracken on the ground; some rocks with juicy moss. Some light fog wafts damp and cold through the trunks.

Toni drags his harp through the woods to a copse. It is mossy and overgrown, with little life-sapping firs. It is deathly quiet.

We see Toni near, his head cocked sideways, strangely, as if he wanted to listen to something. He does not do a thing and remains in the same odd posture.

He gets up, takes his harp, and leans it a few steps away at the other end of the copse. He listens again with his face lifted sideways and does not come to any conclusion.

We hear a bird's voice. Hias appears from out of the tree trunks and abruptly confronts him. Neither of them seems surprised.

HIAS: You are Toni.

TONI: Then you are Hias. 'Cause we've never seen each other, have we?

Toni strokes the harp strings softly, the strings rippling slightly.

TONI: The factory owner's got himself a new glass stove set up.

HIAS: The furnace builders won't come.

TONI: Then I'll go play to the glassblowers.

HIAS: You'll be playing to a madman, I can see it.

Both are quiet, they listen to a bird sing. Hias makes a slight movement with his head.

HIAS: We have the same way to go.

They take off together. They make heavy steps along the wooded slope.

Barn

The hostess has brought a black dog with her to the threshing floor for reassurance. She alerts him to Ascherl and Wudy, who still lie on the ground side by side as before. Both have some hay on their clothes and in their hair.

HOSTESS: X! X! Sic 'em! X! X! X!

The dog crawls and yelps.

HOSTESS: At them! Sic 'em!

The dog looks at her. The hostess takes a pitchfork and threatens the dog. He growls. She beats him across the spine with the pitchfork's handle.

HOSTESS: Bite! At them! Sic—sic 'em! X! X!

She goes on threatening. The dog snarls, barks, and in his dilemma bites Wudy on the arm. Wudy screams.

HOSTESS: Ah, now we know.

She grabs Wudy under the arms and makes him stand up. He makes a sheepish face, unable to figure out what's going on.
The dog wants to bite Wudy's calves. The hostess beats Wudy with the pitchfork.

HOSTESS: What Hias sees happens.

Wudy stares forward without any comprehension whatsoever. Wudy withdraws.
The dog lies down on the threshing floor and licks himself.

Mansion

In the hall, near the broad-curving staircase that leads to an antechamber; a praying chair stands beside the entrance, richly carved in wood. On the wall is a beautiful crucifix. The stove is made of smooth stones. Opposite the end of the stairs, a two-winged door opens out onto the garden.

The glass factory owner kneels on the praying chair, full of devotion, as if absorbed in prayer.

FACTORY OWNER: Glass has an easily breakable soul.
                                  It is unstained.
                                  The Crack is the Besetting Sin.
                                  After the Sin, there is no sound.

VOICE OF ADALBERT: Amen.

The factory owner rises. We now realize that behind him Adalbert has also been kneeling down. He rises too. The factory owner turns to Adalbert slowly. His inspirations come sluggishly forth from his tongue.

FACTORY OWNER: Will the future see the necessary fall of the factories just as we see the mined fortress as a sign of inevitable change?

Adalbert ogles the void for a while.

ADALBERT: People say Hias had seen that nettles are springing out of the glass factories. The lilac bushes will consume themselves for lack of human company, they say.

FACTORY OWNER: The Ruby must save us. Let Muehlbeck's house be torn down and search for the mystery in each and every cranny. The soil whereupon his house stands has to be dug three feet deep. For Muehlbeck could have buried the secret. Bring me the green davenport from Paris, the one he gave to his mother, Anamirl.

Adalbert bows in a wooden fashion and leaves through the door.

The factory owner, near. He ponders.

FACTORY OWNER: The untidiness of the stars makes my head ache.

Death Room

Ascherl is stretched out in a narrow room. The room is painted in a green oil color about shoulder high, and the paint is beginning to peel away. The floor is covered with wet flagstones, which have apparently just been wiped with a pail of water that still stands on the floor.

Paulin puts two candlesticks on each side of the dead man's head and replaces the candles. Paulin hums a foolish song.

She lights the candles. They stand against a small window through which gray daylight penetrates.

Paulin leaves through the door by the feet of the corpse, taking away the bucket and the rag.

The door is closed from without.

The door.

Inn

The innkeeper polishes some glasses behind the counter and is very fussy about it. He watches his guests. They keep still. The door beside the counter opens. The guests don't take note of him; they just stare at each other.

TONI: Here I am.

INNKEEPER: Jeez, Toni! I think this time you've brought us funeral music.

TONI: God, am I thirsty.

INNKEEPER: A wheat beer first, as always.

Toni sits at the table where Wudy and Ascherl always sit. The guests are very oppressive in the way they stare at each other unflinchingly. The innkeeper returns and serves Toni his wheat beer. He takes his seat across from him.

INNKEEPER: They buried Muehlbeck yesterday, our top workman.
  Now they don't know what to do.

TONI: Hias already predicted that.

INNKEEPER: Then you also know the thing about the Ruby.

TONI: The thing with the Ruby is the master's malady.

Mansion

Ludmilla picks up the Ruby mug from the carpet, the factory owner
having taken it from the case in the office. Apparently he just left it
there. Hias steps behind Ludmilla without making a sound.

HIAS: Ludmilla.

  Ludmilla is frightened and drops the mug. We cannot tell if
it is broken.

HIAS: Leave it; there is more to break today.

  Only Ludmilla's face; she looks waxen. Very softly she shows
her joy with Hias's presence.
  Hias carefully places his massive, bandaged arm around her
shoulder.

HIAS: Go away from the mansion. The master could very well slip
  and end up sitting on your face.

  A view of the display case in the adjacent room. Hias is at-
tracted by the case. He steps close and stares at the glass.
  Ludmilla, alone. She has a flushed face.

Office

In the office, there now stands a larger table, not far from the
desk, packed with books. The factory owner sits behind the untidy heap. We look at him with the eyes of Ludmilla, who stands
before him.

The factory owner has something distracted and nasty about him. He looks up.

FACTORY OWNER: What does that whining mean?

Ludmilla sobs.
He lifts his big sackcloth. Boundless weeping.

FACTORY OWNER: It is better for the servants to pray that we
   rediscover the law of the Ruby than to blubber.
LUDMILLA: So much will happen. Hias is outside, you know.

Startled, the glass factory owner goes to the door of a small adjoining reception room and sees stacks of old files and exhibition pieces. Hias stands with his back to us, scratching his head.

FACTORY OWNER: He is here—he knew it! He didn't need a
   messenger!

Hias revolves clumsily. He speaks overly calm and slow, like a threat.

HIAS: The master may send for a hunter to shoot the bear. The bulls
   are frightened, and Sam and I can't guarantee that he won't rip
   a bull to pieces while the others escape. On the Day of the Bear,
   a bull runs as far as Mainz.
FACTORY OWNER: Muehlbeck has died, taking the secret with him,
   but you must find the ingredient for the Ruby glass. Muehlbeck
   has forsaken us.
HIAS: I don't know the ingredient.
FACTORY OWNER: You'd know it for ten florins.

Hias lapses into reflection. He shakes his head.

FACTORY OWNER: Then you'll know it for a thousand.

In the background we can hear Ludmilla cry. The factory owner lapses into trance.

FACTORY OWNER: Do you want our people to have to eat oat bread again, which only gives them a headache?

Hias shakes his head.

FACTORY OWNER: Then tell me the secret so we can produce the Ruby glass again and so you can be master of the factory. I shall carry a millstone to Trier.

HIAS: I am here only as a hunter.

FACTORY OWNER: I want to see the Ruby again! I want the red glass, understand? I need a glass to carry my blood. Or else it will trickle away.

The factory owner has seized Hias by the throat and shakes him.

FACTORY OWNER: The sun is hurting me.

Hias pushes the factory owner away with a jerk.

HIAS: You will never see the sun again. The rats will bite your earlobes.

Shop

It is a kind of grocery or, rather, a small store that apparently belongs to the inn. A simple counter, chests and stacks. Sacks filled with grain on the floor. Through the open door in the background, we recognize an oven.

The innkeeper's wife shovels flour into Hias's sack from a chest. She sets the sack on the counter and ties it.

HOSTESS: Ascherl's dead in the closet.

HIAS: That's the beginning.

HOSTESS: Will you be going up to the woods again?

Hias starts; a vision overcomes him.

HIAS: Wait. I don't need the flour anymore.
HOSTESS: Then I'll pour it back into the chest.

She unties the string and pours the flour back into the chest.
She stops.

HOSTESS: And Sam, doesn't he need any flour?
HIAS: You can see it, too: he is lying under a tree, slain.

The innkeeper's wife dusts the sack and folds it.
Close-up: the sack lying on the counter.

Office

In the office, the factory owner sits at the reading table; we look
at him from the position of Adalbert, who stands in front of him.
Meanwhile the factory owner seems to be pulling some books
to pieces, to search the bindings. Numerous disemboweled and
mangled volumes are lying about.

ADALBERT: The davenport is here.
FACTORY OWNER: Carry it in!

He stiffens. Adalbert holds the door. Two workmen carry in
a green davenport. They deposit it in front of the factory owner.

FACTORY OWNER: I am delighted about this letter. Adalbert, give
    me the opener.

Adalbert takes it from the table where it's still stuck in the
binding of a thick old volume.

FACTORY OWNER: Let's read the message.

The factory owner pokes into the velvet and cuts it. He does the same to the sackcloth. Then he gives the letter opener back to Adalbert. The factory owner rips out the seaweed and rummages the entrails of the davenport until it heaps upon the floor beside him. Adalbert pokes into it with great caution.

FACTORY OWNER: Can you decipher that? If a letter reaches someone with the words scattered around, it should make you think.

Theatrically the factory owner raises his gaze toward Fate, which he tries to find on the ceiling.

FACTORY OWNER: You are sending me letters I don't understand. But everything I need can be had for nothing; only the superfluous things cost money.

Garden

Again the picture unravels with light, as in old films. We see an image that has the tranquillity and harmony of very old photos. Hias is resting beneath a fruit tree; we overlook the countryside with him. It is autumn. If we look closer, the idyllic scene seems chilly.

Hias sings softly and out of tune while gazing distantly.

HIAS: (in dialect)
    Koa Huettenmadel mog I met,
    Die hot koa dicke Wadl net,
    I suach mir a Madl aus der Slodt
    Die wo dicke Wadl hot . . .

Glass Factory

A long, moving view around the furnace. The glassblowers work again and perform a wonderful and mysterious ballet. The furnace glows. The glass lumps dance, trailing white blazing traces in the room. The masters blow on the pipes as on the choicest musical instruments. An enormous activity, always under the pressure of time to finish the piece before it has cooled too much to be molded properly. They drink beer in heavy drafts. The men are sweating; the hands work with their wooden molds. With a pair of tongs, someone pinches a glass lump held by the master; a handle appears. The glass is a wondrously pliable matter; it is sheer delight to watch it. Hasty movement between the cooling furnace and the platform. Magic shadows stray along the walls. The glowing holes glow. A master blower blows a still-shapeless little balloon into the closing mold in his hand; it is steaming; the master blows, turns it, and examines it. In a whitish blue, a mug is forming. We see Agide going around the platform.

AGIDE (shouting): Lunchtime, men! Take 'em off!

The activity slowly subsides, flickering away. Some heads turn toward the entrance to the hall. We see the factory owner entering the factory. In the doorway he wrings his hands. He holds his hands up to his face, as if he were hiding something joyous. He bursts into the factory. Not all of the glassblowers have seen him yet. Some of them are just finishing their last pieces, and the bearers carry them to the cooling oven.

FACTORY OWNER (wriggling): I have it.

He spreads his arms.

FACTORY OWNER: All of us.

His hands travel all over his body.

FACTORY OWNER: It's there inside. (Touching his forehead.) There, too!

He strokes his calf. He makes a far-reaching gesture, and all of a sudden he runs forward a little, leaps into the air, and falls

down in the dust. Whitish remnants of potash whirl up. They help him get up; they surround him. Everyone presses in on him.
Hias is among them.

FACTORY OWNER (out of breath): I've sent for the oven builders at Ploessberg.

ALL: Hurrah!

The factory owner is carried out in triumph; only a few stay in the factory. We see Agide together with Gigl.

AGIDE: The mistress will be surprised when she returns from her trip.

Abruptly, Hias comes between them; his vision sounds hoarse.

HIAS: You will see nothing intact when she comes back.

GIGL: Lunatic!

HIAS: When the mistress jumps from the carriage, she will fall into the mud, because there's no one there to meet her, and you will be on a big boat, puking.

GIGL (sarcastically): Anything else?

AGIDE: How about a free beer today?

HIAS: Yes.

Anamirl's House

Anamirl is standing at the door of her little wooden house. A small flower bed of asters in front of it. At a window, a wooden box with withered fuchsias.
Hias goes toward her.

HIAS: Your son has died.

Anamirl goes into the house. Hias follows her.
Inside. We see from the hall into the living room. It is a nar-

row, cozy room with tiny windows. A tiled stove with a bench. Everything is arranged in a rather cluttered manner, with the exception of a distinct gap where the davenport used to be.

HIAS: They have carried away your davenport.

In the room, Hias sits down at the table. Anamirl keeps still, a sustained, friendly silence. From her manner toward Hias, we gather that she's known him a long time. From a sideboard near the chimney, Anamirl takes out two pieces of a broken pottery bowl. She sets them on the table below the Lord's Corner. From the table drawer she takes a crust of bread and puts it beside them.

HIAS: That bowl, there; that was them, too.

Hias grabs a piece and takes a bite from the crust, chews the bread, and sticks the chewed bread into the crack.

Anamirl stands opposite, propping herself on the table with one hand, watching Hias. Both sink into mute reflection.

After Hias has glued the entire crack with bread, he puts the two broken pieces together, holds the bowl against his body, takes a burnt wire from his pocket, and puts it around the bowl. He takes a pair of tongs from his pocket, ties the wire, and cuts off the ends. He puts the rest of the wire and tools back into his trouser pockets.

Anamirl winds the end of the wire into her other hand, carries it to the stove, and throws it into the logs. It is like some work that they've always done together. Anamirl takes a pan of milk from the cupboard and sets it on the table in front of Hias, who meanwhile has started to eat up the bread crust. Hias broods; he chews; his jaws are moving slowly.

Anamirl watches him.

HIAS: When night falls, vision dies. Many things come to pass. But the rain never falls upward.

Hias has finished and leaves without a word. He closes the door behind him.

From inside, the door.

Mansion

The dining room.

A large table with eight chairs around it. The factory owner sits at the head of the table. All the other chairs are empty, except one. There still sits the glassblower Wenzel, with his heavy leather apron, and a heavy, shiny glove beside his plate. He doesn't get on very well with his knife and fork and is embarrassed. Apparently he was invited as a special favor and has been pressed to eat dinner at the table. As the factory owner has finished, Wenzel pretends to have finished, too, although his plate is half-filled. The factory owner stretches in his chair in a kind of euphoria. He wipes his mouth with a napkin. Wenzel copies him.

Ludmilla nimbly puts the china on the platter. It is very elegant china, almost royal, much like the room's furniture.

FACTORY OWNER: Your prayer has caused a miracle. An hour ago I learned something I never knew before: I can sell my secret to every glass factory.

Ludmilla drops something. She is very distracted.

FACTORY OWNER: Break as much as you can. I am going to let ten racks of Ruby glass be carried up Mount Arber and have it thrown into the lake so the water turns red. Adalbert! Did my servant get that?

Adalbert steps up to the dining table with a notebook and pencil.

Anamirl's House

The door of Anamirl's living room inside.

Rumbling.

The door opens from outside, and two workmen carry in Anamirl's davenport. Anamirl appears and swiftly removes a chair. They put the davenport in its proper place.

WORKMAN: There, Anamirl, now you can sit softly again.

The second one counts ten florins on the table.

SECOND WORKMAN: If you need more money sometime, we'll fetch the davenport again for the master to poke a hole in, and he'll give you another ten florins.

The two men exit.
Anamirl fetches a little tablecloth from under her bench to put on the spot where the davenport has been opened up. She smoothes it over, then leaves through the door.

It is dark in the hallway. She opens the front door. The sunlight floods in. Anamirl goes out and is forced to sneeze.

Ten men pass by; we see them from the front door, each carrying a rack filled with glass on his back. They pass with weighty, stamping steps, like a death ballet. Against the light, they are like an engraving. Not a word is uttered.

Mansion

Ludmilla is standing behind a lower window of the kitchen. We see Hias walk toward her from the orchard. Ludmilla opens the window.

LUDMILLA: The master's out of order.

HIAS: In the factory he's been Beelzebub.

Ludmilla instinctively makes the sign of the cross.

HIAS: He sent ten men with racks of glass into the woods. But since they are not stupid enough to throw the valuable glass into the lake, they'll smuggle it over the border and sell it. Ludmilla, leave before he imposes his will on you.

From the background we hear the voice of Adalbert.

ADALBERT: Ludmilla, dress up by five o'clock. The master desires
    your company.

LUDMILLA (frightened): Hias!

Adalbert appears beside Ludmilla at the window.

ADALBERT: I have to take care of the music.

HIAS: There will be someone coming up the path who can play the
    radleier, the hurdy-gurdy.

ADALBERT: I'd have to sing to the *radleier*.

HIAS: Harp Toni is sitting in the inn.

ADALBERT: Tell him to come. It won't do him any harm.

Ludmilla hesitatingly withdraws from the window into the
interior of the kitchen.

Hias crosses the orchard to the gravel path, where a stranger
with a bundle awaits him. Under the trees, great quantities of
apples have not been collected. They ferment. Hias leaves with
the stranger.

Mansion

It is a completely frenzied sleepwalking scene, which has a stranger
effect due to the somnambulistic harp music.

The factory owner sits in his easy chair, arms resting on the
armrests, and is fully carried away. Toni plays a fantasy on the
harp.

Ludmilla sits on a stool in the middle of the room like a calf.
Adalbert is standing by the door.

The factory owner rises. Toni shuts his eyes and plays. Ludmilla
keeps her hands in her lap, as if she were cold.

Adalbert remains inscrutable. The factory owner steps to the
fireplace behind his chair and gazes into the fire. Adalbert closes
the door of the adjoining room behind Toni.

Ludmilla is weeping.

Adalbert takes his place by the door.

The factory owner walks over to the sword on the wall beside the chimney.

The harp ripples. Ludmilla weeps loudly into her hands. A painting drops from the wall.

Toni looks up.

Adalbert takes the picture and leans it against the wall.

Ludmilla jumps up and runs to the door.

Adalbert removes the key and steps inside. Ludmilla tugs at the handle. The factory owner examines the sword's blade with his thumb.

The row of ancestors, among them the empty space of the fallen painting.

Ludmilla screams. Toni stops playing.

The factory owner draws the sword from its sheath.

Toni resumes playing.

Adalbert plays with the door key, as he isn't sure whether to put it back in the lock to open it or not.

Landscape

The picture opens in a circle, but it doesn't show the whole screen. As in old photographs, we have a round section of landscape set within a rectangular frame. There are dark woods on the hill, one behind the other: Mount Osser, the Lusen, Mount Rachel. The sun sinks behind the woods. A perfect, lamentable harmony.

And a panic-stricken scream from Ludmilla.

Sounds of sipping, as if someone were drinking without a cup. The picture narrows to a point and leaves us in darkness for a moment.

Inn

Inside the inn there is great turmoil. By and by we realize that a kind of strange and collective madness is breaking out. It is not noticeable all at once, but we feel it gradually.

Hias and a stranger, his bundle on the table, sit by themselves in a corner. Hias is isolated from the other men. He is completely introverted; he doesn't notice anything around him. The prophecies drag out of him.

STRANGER: And then?

HIAS: Then the Little One starts a War, and the Big One across the ocean extinguishes it. Then you won't get a loaf of bread for two hundred florins. Then a strict master comes, who will pull people's heads up over their heads, with their skins. After the War you think there will be Peace, but there won't be.

Paulin lights the candles on the tables. The faces light up, flushed. At the bar the men are standing with beer mugs in their hands; they have quiet and enchanted faces.

We see Wudy at his usual spot; he is tearful.

WUDY: I miss Ascherl.

AGIDE: You shouldn't have smothered him.

WUDY: Ascherl should be with us today.

AGIDE: Then you will have to go out and join him. He can't come in.

WUDY: Bring me some Ascherl.

Wudy shoves himself away from the table and gets up from his bench. He exits.

We see Hias with the stranger again.

HIAS: Believe or don't believe—that's your affair. I say what I see. Whether it comes to pass, I don't know.

STRANGER: Yes, all right, and then?

HIAS: The farmers will dress up like townspeople. And the townspeople will be like apes. The women wear trousers and boots. The farmers will stand on their dung heaps with polished shoes. The farmers will eat cake and talk politics.

Wudy returns. He carries dead Ascherl on his shoulders.

There is quiet expectancy. Only Gigl seems to be unaffected.

GIGL: Quit that lunacy!

WUDY: Who's gonna play us some dance music?

The stranger rises.

STRANGER: I'll play for this couple here.

He takes a *radleier* from his bundle, goes to the bar, and plays dance music.

Wudy relieves himself of the stiff Ascherl, hugs him, and starts to dance with him. The onlookers make gestures of religious frenzy.

Mansion

Meanwhile, the glass factory owner has been overcome by a serene, relaxed kind of madness. He feels the arm of the stabbed Ludmilla on the floor.

FACTORY OWNER: She'll be cooled off soon, and then she won't break anymore.

He lifts her. Adalbert opens the door. The factory owner carries Ludmilla out in his arms. Adalbert follows. The door remains open.

Crashing of broken glass.

Toni awakes from his swoon in a state of semiconsciousness. He resumes playing the fantasy on his harp. His glance wanders to the empty easy chair with no comprehension, then to the empty stool, then to the open door. He now closes his eyes while playing.

The factory owner comes back alone. He steps to the big pool of blood on the floor. He pulls off his ruffled shirt and soaks it in blood.

FACTORY OWNER: This is the pure mixture. What good are factories anymore?

He has difficulty putting on his shirt, having turned one sleeve inside out. He slips into the sleeves as they are. From the fireplace he takes a burning log. When he passes Harp Toni with it, Toni opens his eyes. Like someone waking from a hypnotic sleep, his perception, his intelligence, and his state of orientation return to him. Full of terror, Toni jumps into the strings of his harp, tumbles down with it, and can't free himself properly.

The factory owner leaves the room with the log.

Adalbert enters and spots Toni, who is fighting his instrument, then shakes his head with the indignation of a domestic. He seems to think this untidiness is indecent. He takes the stool and sets it in front of the fallen picture, steps on the stool, and hangs up the ancestor. He steps back to examine if the picture hangs straight. He puts back the stool.

He leaves the room. The door remains open. We can hear him calling from outside.

ADALBERT: Ludmilla! A pail with water and a rag to wipe the floor!

Thus he deadens the ugly sounds of the harp.

Village

The village lies in the dark; there is hardly any light in the windows. The factory owner drifts through the dark in pursuit of the flaming log in his hands. Some distant shouting and strains of music blow over from the inn.

The factory owner heads toward the glass factory. We recognize in the light of his torch that he finds the entrance door locked. The burning log vanishes behind the glass factory.

Inn

Hias sits at a table by himself.

At the bar in the background, we overhear a fight over whether or not everyone should continue to let Wudy play around with Ascherl.

Apparently only Gigl wants him to stop. The *radleier* is playing and stopping again.

Hias, closer; he is Complete Introspection.

HIAS: Everyone is building; they build and they build everywhere, endless rows, they build them like beehives. In the city they build houses with five and six stories; everywhere they build houses like castles and vicarages and schools like palaces. And the number of people goes up, not down.

Hias stops; no one has listened to him.

GIGL: Let the dead rest! Stop raving!

FIRST VOICE: Paulin's gonna dance!

SECOND VOICE: She'll dance on the table, naked!

HIAS: They make laws and impose taxes, those gentlemen, but no one can pay, and nobody cares anymore. Many things are decided but not carried out. The Lords sit together and invent taxes and laws. And then the people rise up.

THIRD VOICE: Over here; there's room on Hias's table.

HIAS: One will come after the other.

The same view of Hias. Around and by him people sit down, madness etched upon their faces. They take no notice of Hias; they only notice Paulin.

THIRD VOICE: All right, Paulin, up on the table! Up!

We only see Paulin's bare feet on the tabletop, not far from Hias's hands. Someone pushes Hias's beer mug aside to make more room. While Hias talks on, one by one, scraps of clothing fall to the table.

HIAS: They all fight. Whoever has something will be robbed of it. There is war in every house. No man can help the other anymore. The rich and elegant people will be murdered. Whoever has smooth hands will be slain. The farmers will put high fences around their houses and shoot at the townspeople from their windows. The townspeople beg, "Let me plow the ground," but they will be slain. No man will like another man. When two are sitting on the same bench and one of them says, "Move over," and the other doesn't, it will be his death. That will be the time of the Clearing of the Benches.

We follow Hias's gaze as it travels up to naked Paulin. Paulin hasn't a single hair on her body, with which she confronts the frenzied people. Hias continues talking with face upturned.

HIAS: You won't be able to tell the difference between summer and winter; everybody will have a different head. And the forest will get sparse like the beggar's gown. The small shall be tall again.
FOURTH VOICE: You there with the instrument, keep playin'!
THIRD VOICE: Dance, Paulin!

A polka. Paulin lifts the soles of her feet, but timidly.

HIAS: When the Redcoats come with their red coats, you'll have to run away as fast as you can, and take care that you carry a loaf of bread. Whoever has three loaves and drops one on the way mustn't bend.

The music speeds up. Paulin's feet dance more swiftly.

HIAS: Even when you lose the second loaf, you must leave it behind, because you're in such a hurry, and you can subsist on just one loaf since things won't last long. He who survives must have an iron head. People get sick, and no one can help them. The few who survive will greet each other as Brother and Sister.
VOICE IN DOORWAY: Fire! The factory is on fire! Fire!

All run to the window and to the door. Big clamor. The faces are lit by the fire's glow. Some jump through the windows; the others press toward the door. Scolding, curses, cries of pain. Through the confusion we briefly see the blazing flames. From two windows the flames shoot up symmetrically.

Hias sits alone in the empty inn. Only Paulin is standing by the table, and she dresses herself in total tranquillity.

The candles and the inferno together result in a two-way flicker. Through the open window, screaming and crackling penetrate. Hias watches Paulin dress and speaks.

HIAS: People make themselves at home as if they didn't want to leave this world, ever. But overnight the Clearing of the World begins.

Hias pulls out his knife, and while he's elaborating he carves something into the table, something that could be the Bavarian Forest, the Danube, the Rhine, or even England.

HIAS: A snake of the lowest army of Redcoats comes across the woods and up the Danube, headed for the Rhine like the other army lines. Now there are so many doves that rise from the sand, I can't count them. They drop a large black box over the headquarters. There is a larger spot where nothing is alive anymore—no man, no animal, no grass. No soldier of the three army lines shall survive. From the Orient, a huge bird appears and shits into the sea. The sea rises as high as a house and boils. The earth trembles, and a big island half-drowns. The big city with the iron tower is in flames. But the fire was started by the people themselves. And the city is leveled to the ground. In Italy, the Clergy are murdered and the churches collapse. The Pope is sitting in a cell. During his flight he consecrates a goat as bishop. The people are starving. The three days of darkness draw nearer. When the black box drops, a green and yellow dust arises. The poor people turn black, and their flesh peels off their bones. The weather will change. Vineyards will be grown in our region, and unfamiliar fruit.

We hear Adalbert calling "Ludmilla!" outside, the shouts coming closer and closer.

Adalbert comes into the inn; he's so utterly out of his senses that he could be called almost normal again.

ADALBERT: Is Ludmilla here?

He sees the open windows and closes them authoritatively, one after another.

ADALBERT: Ludmilla!

He takes a beer mug that had tumbled to the floor and puts it on the counter.
Hias rises. The dimwit Paulin is beside him.

HIAS: Ludmilla is lying dead in the master's office. Toni is playing her one piece after another on the harp.

Office

A faint flicker from the factory inferno permeates the office and turns the room into a place with an atmosphere of specters and horror. Toni plays the harp.
We now see Ludmilla in the darkness on the floor amid broken glass. Now and again some light flits over her.
The door opens slowly. Adalbert sneaks in with a candle in his hand. He looks about, catches sight of Ludmilla. He draws her away from the broken glass by her leg, puts her dress in order, crosses her hands on her breast, and puts the candle at her head. He tiptoes out and closes the door behind him.

Inn

Hias is sitting by himself in the inn. It is a loneliness without consolation. When the earlier patrons come in again, he wants to leave. They grab him by the shirt.

PATRONS: Stay here. They say it's you who's done this to us!

More and more men appear. In their madness they need a victim.

PATRONS: You've wished for our bad luck. You're to blame.

HIAS: I have only foreseen it.

VOICES: Then tear out his eyes! The Devil's Eyes! The Evil Eye!

GIGL: C'mon, men, don't make such a fuss. We'll bind him now and deliver him to justice.

They bind him, tie his legs and wrists together, and carry him out. They manage him with considerable effort, as Hias is very heavy. In the hallway we see people beating him up.

Hias is thrown into the closet, where Ascherl has been carelessly disposed of.

The door is closed.

The candles have nearly melted down.

Rumbling and scolding from outside.

Prison

We behold a gloomy cell. Chains and neck rings on the wall, some primitive wooden beds with straw mattresses beginning to rot. No windows. The weak light descends dismally from somewhere above.

Hias and the glass factory owner are locked up together. Hias, the trapped animal, is pacing up and down. The factory owner cowers on the floor, yet he seems filled with serenity.

Hias pounds the damp stones with his fist.

HIAS: I can't see anymore! I want to go back to the woods! I want to see something again!

FACTORY OWNER: Yet you don't want to see a soul, I like you. You have a heart of glass.

Forest

Again the picture lights up from a point. Mount Arber seen from the Rabenstein. On the very top, a thin layer of virgin snow has settled on the gloomy woods. Somber clouds and a biting wind. The woods are chanting with frost. We see Hias marching through the underbrush and the storm. He carries a blanket around his shoulders; he ascends lightly and swiftly, freed of a burden.

Hias catches sight of the entrance to a cave. He creeps in; our eyes follow him. It is getting dark. We overhear the snarling of a raging bear. Stillness.

We behold the entrance to the cave. Hastily, Hias comes back out. Now a very strange scene is taking place. Hias pulls out his knife.

Behind him an imaginary bear creeps out of the cave and attacks him. Hias crashes down and fights the beast in a battle of life and death. Hias looks like the Laocoön group without the serpent. Now the bear holds him in a clinch. Hias succeeds in freeing his right hand with the knife. He sticks his knife into the sides of the imaginary beast. The bear dies. Hias frees himself completely from its clutches.

For a moment he catches his breath, and he sees that he's not seriously injured. He gathers some twigs and lights a little fire.

HIAS: And now for some roasted bear.

But Hias doesn't do anything. He stares into the fire and warms himself. Something is fermenting inside Hias; slowly and haltingly, he finds the language.

HIAS: In the night someone looks across the forest and doesn't see a single light. When he sees a juniper bush in twilight, he goes to see if it is a human being, there are so few of them left. In the woods the roosters are crowing, but the people have perished.

Hias's face becomes overjoyed, as he sees something very clearly and palpably.

HIAS: Something else occurs to me! I see it again: a coachman
knocks on the ground with his whip and says, "There once
was this big Straubinger town—"

At once a Great Music swells up.
Starting from a point on the screen, a picture unravels in a
circle. The woods, the mountains seen from Hias's viewpoint. It
is, as before, the great quietude of the earliest photographs.
The sun descends below the frozen Mount Falkenstein.

Werner Herzog was born in Munich and grew up in a remote mountain village in Bavaria, where he never saw films, television, or telephones as a child. During high school he worked the night shift as a welder in a steel factory and made his first film in 1961 at the age of nineteen. Since then, he has produced, written, and directed more than seventy films, including *Nosferatu the Vampyre* and *Grizzly Man*; published more than a dozen books of prose; and directed many operas. His books *Scenarios* and *Of Walking in Ice* have also been published by the University of Minnesota Press.

Krishna Winston is Marcus L. Taft Professor of German Language and Literature at Wesleyan University.